LONE PINE
IN THE MOVIES

WHERE THE REAL WEST BECOMES THE REEL WEST

Packy Smith
—publisher

Ed Hulse
—editor

Michael Bifulco
—design & page production

Richard W. Bann
—contributing editor

Elizabeth Gulick
—cover design

Don Kelsen
—special photography

Lone Pine in the Movies is published by the Beverly and Jim Rogers Lone Pine Film History Museum, 701 South Main Street, Lone Pine CA 93545. Published in conjunction with the 2013 Lone Pine Film Festival. The contents of this issue are copyright © 2013 by the Beverly and Jim Rogers Film History Museum. All rights reserved. Nothing in this magazine may be reprinted in whole or in part, in any media or format, without prior written permission from the publisher and/or the copyright holder.

Special Thanks to: Richard W. Bann, Don Kelsen, Billy King, Don Murray, Sam Sherman, Packy Smith.

Photo and Art Acknowledgments: All stills, posters, and lobby cards reprinted in these pages are copyright © their respective years of publication by Columbia Pictures Corporation, Monogram Pictures Corporation, Paramount Pictures, Twentieth Century-Fox Film Corporation, Victory Pictures Corporation, and their respective successors in interest. Photos shot for "Photographic Treasure Hunting" are copyright © 2013 by Don Kelsen and used here with his permission.

Introduction

by Ed Hulse

Welcome to the all-Westerns issue of *Lone Pine in the Movies*, which celebrates its tenth anniversary this year. When I self-published the first issue in 2003, I had no idea if it would find a receptive audience. It was offered for sale at that year's Lone Pine Film Festival and, to my surprise and delight, was snapped up by nearly three hundred eager buyers. The magazine's success inspired me to publish several more issues, each released in conjunction with the annual Film Festival, and eventually *Lone Pine in the Movies* was underwritten by the Beverly and Jim Rogers Lone Pine Film History Museum. Unfortunately, the early numbers are now out of print, but those published from 2009 on are available both from Amazon and at the Museum gift shop. (You can also buy copies on line at the Museum web site, lonepinefilmhistorymuseum.org.)

Although Film Festival attendees get first crack at each new issue, I realize that many of you purchase the magazine on line, or while visiting the Museum when passing through Lone Pine. That's why I urge you to consider joining us one October for the big show. Our yearly celebration of movies made here has become a must-attend event for hundreds of film fans, and 2013's Film Festival will be the 24th consecutive confab. In nearly a quarter century of such events we have been graced with the presence of such stars as Gregory Peck, Douglas Fairbanks Jr., Roy Rogers, Clayton Moore, Ernest Borgnine, and Lash LaRue, to name just a handful off the top of my head. Veteran producers, directors and screenwriters who have visited our Festival include Budd Boetticher, Burt Kennedy, A. C. Lyles, and William Witney. Their participation has added a great deal to our understanding and appreciation of the filmmaking process, especially as it relates to Lone Pine and the Eastern Sierras.

Attending the Film Festival requires a significant commitment of time and money, but we enjoy the support of many, many people who make the trip year after year. Some build their annual vacation around the Festival, which unfolds every October on the weekend before Columbus Day is celebrated. Why do they do it? One gentleman explained it to me several years ago. "This sort of thing is probably old hat to you guys who live and breathe old movies," he said, "but for me it's an opportunity I could never have dreamed of. Every year I come here, watch movies made here, then go out and visit the spots they were made on, and listen to the people who made them. How can you beat that?"

Strictly speaking, you *can't* beat it. That's what makes the Lone Pine Film Festival unique among the many events and venues where vintage motion pictures are shown and studied. Nowhere else can you watch an old Western and afterward, following a five- or ten-minute drive into the Alabama Hills, find yourself standing exactly where that Western's cast and crew stood when they were making the horse opera as much as 60, 70 or 80 years ago. Lone Pine is still an active movie location—in recent years, parts of *Iron Man* and *Django Unchained* were shot here—but our Film Festival and Film History Museum venerate motion pictures produced in this area many, many decades in the past. In another few

Film Festival attendees studying a location in the Alabama Hills.

years we'll be celebrating Lone Pine's centennial as a location for Hollywood filmmakers. Until then, the Film Festival continues to honor the achievements of those actors, writers, directors, and stuntmen who labored so hard, and often under difficult conditions, to create the entertaining works that have so enriched America's popular culture.

This issue's cover story features Richard W. Bann's reportage on last year's visit from Don Murray, who starred in one of the most unusual Westerns ever made up here: *From Hell to Texas* (1958), directed by the great Henry Hathaway, a veteran of Lone Pine location work. I had the pleasure of conducting a one-on-one interview with Don after last year's sold-out Festival screening of *From Hell to Texas*, and Dick's lengthy article includes most of the highlights from our discussion. But reading it is no substitute for hearing it live, as last year's audience members can tell you.

By the time most of you purchase this magazine, the 2013 Film Festival will have come and gone. But next year's event will be a very special one: our Silver Anniversary. Why not join us for what promises to be a most memorable weekend? You can keep track of our preparations—the naming of

guests, the addition of panel discussions, and the choosing of films to be shown—at the Festival web site, www.lonepinefilmfestival.org.

In the meantime, I hope this issue of *Lone Pine in the Movies* offers you several hours of reading pleasure.   ☐☐☐

Don Murray speaking with Ed Hulse.

AN APPRECIATION OF THE LONE PINE FILM FESTIVAL

The annual gathering of movie fans who spend an entire weekend watching films made locally and visiting the locations on which they were shot.

by Richard W. Bann

Film historian Richard W. Bann.

Every year, the Lone Pine Film Festival offers visitors a wonderful retreat. The appeal is basic and uncomplicated. For anyone arriving in this small desert town, attention is absolutely transfixed by the awe-inspiring sight of dominant Mount Whitney, the highest point in the contiguous United States. The magnificent snow-capped Sierra Nevada mountain range remains a natural wonder, unchanged through millenniums.

It's hard to resist racing right up into the equally remarkable and immense rock formations of those breathtaking Alabama Hills, just beneath the skyline. The enormous granite boulders there cast shadows offering amazingly different and dynamic views depending on time of day, and where the sun is, or isn't. It's not surprising that filmmakers have always found Lone Pine a versatile setting. The place is quiet and still, but full of surprise. Every Lone Pine pilgrimage defies us all not to see ghosts—the phantom spirits of long-gone movie cowboys. Just think of your own favorites traversing the canyons, passes and winding trails: They've all been here.

The Alabama Hills Inn was built two decades ago to accommodate Mel Gibson's company while shooting scenes for his remake of *Maverick*. At festival time in October, I always stay there, and purposely walk into town each day. And then back again through the cool night air, listening to the soothing sounds of cattle grazing on the venerable Anchor Ranch, beneath a display of stars in a smog-free, clear sky. Year after year I take the same guided bus tours of filmmaking locations, enjoying the running commentaries of our guides, some of them live and some recorded. Their enthusiasm and sense of wonder are contagious. I've even started guiding tours myself.

Each year it's fun finding collectibles for sale from a variety of vendors in Statham Hall and at the park. In past years I mingled with cheerful vendors like Jerry Rosenthal and Grace Bradley Boyd, representing Hopalong Cassidy licensed merchandise, and Cheryl Rogers Barnett, representing her late parents, Roy Rogers and Dale Evans. Burly Mitch Schaperkotter sold rare Lone Pine-lensed Westerns on videotape, and Las Vegas-based Ray Dennis Steckler, himself a filmmaker with a cult following, offered movie memorabilia. Nowadays you can find some of the guest stars selling autographed stills at Statham Hall alongside film historians peddling recent books they've written.

While not officially on the leisurely Film Festival program, one worthwhile activity is driving way, way up near Whitney Portal to explore the forested pond there, cool off by the mountain stream, and study the incredible view with friends. I look forward to our hearty, happily high-fat, artery-clogging breakfasts at the local cafés—meals that everyone works off with ease while strolling around town and climbing rocks in the Alabama Hills. The Friday-night concert invariably satisfies, although some years more than others.

Every year it's good to visit the "Hoppy cabin" up on Tuttle Creek Road, each time relating the experience to the most recent screening of some Western shot there—maybe *Renegade Trail* (1939) or *Bar 20 Rides Again* (1935). After the colorful midday parade on Sunday, a bunch of us, guys and gals alike, depart for the rugged environs of Movie Road and "Lone Ranger Canyon," where we ride horses for hours until we're all sore. Caked with dust, half crippled, and really sore.

So many of us just feel at home in Lone Pine, doing simple things in the company of friends who share the same appreciation for all these unpretentious attractions and activities. Seems good for the soul. Maybe because it represents the fulfillment of dreams we all had as kids, watching the movies made in Lone Pine and aching to get here, long before we knew where "here" was.

Lots of people work hard to produce this event year after year, yet somehow they make it look effortless. The Film Festival is nicely low key, and rests at just the right level of organized activity. Along with the

The "Hoppy Cabin" in 1938.

traditional values indigenous to the films we celebrate, there is a refreshing lack of modern relevance here, or any kind of hip progressiveness—the kind one finds increasingly at film festivals in places such as Sundance or Telluride. So far Lone Pine has been able to resist commercial and "progressive" ideas. Cancer is something else that's progressive, and we don't need any more of that, either. People clearly like Lone Pine just the way it is, because it's still just the way it was. No "improvements" appear to be necessary. Is anyone yet arguing for revisions in, or another misguided remake of, either *Gunga Din* or *High Sierra*? No. They got it right the first time. We wouldn't tamper with the Lone Pine Film Festival either.

Because they live here, the Film Festival organizers may not realize that the basically unchanged, small-town, old-time ambiance is one of the event's principal attractions. Those of us who travel from around the world to meet in Lone Pine, appreciate imagining that all this is essentially the same experience that peerless cowboy aces such as Gene Autry, Roy Rogers and the rest of those pioneer range heroes would have found, when they came here originally to work—when they drove four hours north, out of Los Angeles and through the wilderness, to make the films that bring some of us back here year after year. Because alighting in Lone Pine is really like walking onto the screen, and into a scene from anyone of hundreds of familiar westerns, ranging from Tom Mix's *Flaming Guns* (1932) to Tim Holt's *Arizona Ranger* (1948) to Randolph Scott's *Ride Lonesome* (1959).

Specifically, entering the town from the south side, one immediately expects to see hotheaded Johnny Nelson galloping across "The Great Bar 20 Range," as a text title tells us in the famous series' entry number one, *Hop-a-long Cassidy* (1935). It's a site that is priceless because the panorama looks just as it did all those years ago. We were not here then, but visiting and finding it's all still the same is the next best thing.

We are lucky to be able to revisit these incomparably scenic and nostalgic locations, these tangible connections to the movie-cowboy role models who influenced so many of us, who gave us our values, our sense of morality. That is truly Lone Pine's magic drawing power. Notwithstanding the classic adventure films in which the Alabama Hills have stood in for India, Afghanistan, Burma, and Tibet (among other exotic parts of the world), it is the humble horse operas that link many of us to this hallowed ground. Personally, my favorite Festival activity is boarding the time machine to view these grade-"B" Westerns made right in the neighborhood. Because so many of them were shot in Lone Pine, the Festival particularly celebrates "B" Westerns produced in the pre-TV era.

Lone Pine has no "picture show" theater today. There once was, however, a small "neighborhood house" which served the area, the first of two. This emporium was known as Pearson's Movie Theater, and dated as far back as the early 1920s. It stood for at least half a century, being razed shortly after 1970. We have anecdotal confirmation about this from Joy Anderson, daughter of local rancher Russell Spainhower. He furnished horses and cattle to movie companies and owned the Anchor Ranch, where remnants of the *Gunga Din* sets were used to construct the Spanish mission-and-hacienda complex we know from so many Tim Holt and Hopalong Cassidy westerns.

Mrs. Anderson remembered viewing silent movies in this little theater, located at the intersection of Jackson and Bush Streets, on the present site of the subsequently erected Statham Hall, which today doubles as the dealers' room during the festival. Joy Anderson had vivid memories of reading from the screen text titles used to convey information and dialogue in silent movies. During the 1930s and '40s, 35mm film product was supplied for Lone Pine's movie theater not only by the distribution arms of major studios like M-G-M and RKO, but also by so-called "state-rights" distributors on behalf of smaller, independent, "Gower Gulch" producers releasing through such companies as Monogram, Tiffany, and Victory. Lone Pine and other Inyo County residents caught up with some of these Poverty Row pictures by way of the substandard 16mm film format. Traveling roadshowmen would project 16mm prints, either at Pearson's or against the side of a building, or even upon a suspended white sheet at night!

It's at least possible that one of the 16mm collector-owned prints we run today—an ancient, fragile member of an endangered species—was the same 16mm copy some itinerant exhibitor brought to

project in Lone Pine 60 to 70 years ago! It hardly matters that the probability of this being true is the same likelihood of actually glimpsing Jimmy Ellison racing across the Anchor Ranch as any of us drive into town. But hold onto your dreams. What else are movies for?

The only Festival treat to top such screenings (followed by spontaneous excursions into the Alabams to visit corresponding locations) is the opportunity to meet and converse with the stars and directors of movies shot at Lone Pine. Our chances to convene with authentic Lone Pine Pioneers, however, are dwindling fast. We were able to welcome Roy Rogers and his frequent director, Bill Witney (now both gone), but not Bill Boyd or his frequent director, Lesley Selander. Luckily, leading lady Peggy Stewart has been here often, but her contemporary Carol Hughes never made it. Sadly, it is too late for many. In fact it is too late to honor most of those with an authentic and legitimate connection to the classic films made locally-as well as to the humble, unpretentious Saturday-matinee programmers shot in and around the Alabama Hills during the 1920s, '30s, and '40s. That's why it's important to attend every Lone Pine Film Festival: Our window of opportunity, as it relates to the stars and directors of our favorite films, is gradually drawing shut. Past Festivals have given us wonderful memories, and we can be confident that future shows will do the same.   ☐☐☐

Jack Randall, Rider of the Dawn

Three of the best movies featuring this minor Western star were shot in Lone Pine.

by Ed Hulse

Practically every movie cowboy worked in Lone Pine at least once, and some so many times that it's difficult to visualize them anywhere but in the Alabama Hills, with Mount Whitney and the mighty Sierras beyond. At least a few of cinema's sons of the sage, however, worked here just two or three times. One of these was Jack Randall, whose Westerns helped fill the yearly release schedule of Monogram Pictures Corporation during the late Thirties. A minor star back then, and forgotten today by all but a few hardy horse-opera aficionados, he rarely ventured north of the San Fernando Valley to make his inexpensive starring vehicles, but when he did the results were exceptional.

Addison Owen Randall was born in San Fernando, California, on May 12, 1906. His family had moved to the Golden State from Quincy, Illinois, not long after the birth of Ad's older brother Robert. The elder Randall was a good newspaperman but apparently a bad husband. The boys' parents eventually divorced, and Bob and Ad were sent back to Quincy to live with relatives. Both were tall, dark and handsome lads who readily found favor with lassies, and they had women trouble throughout their lives.

The brothers returned to Southern California as young men and sought employment as actors. They wangled work as extras on the M-G-M lot, where Bob stayed. He became a Metro contract player in 1934 and changed his surname to Livingston. Ad, who called himself Jack Randall for billing purposes, landed a contract with RKO Radio in 1935 and appeared in a number of pictures for that company—including the 1936 Astaire-Rogers musical *Follow the Fleet*—but always in supporting roles.

Bob Livingston left M-G-M in 1936 to play "Stony Brooke" in a new Western series based on the "Three Mesquiteers" pulp-fiction novels written by William Colt MacDonald. It was produced by Nat Levine for the recently formed Republic Pictures Corporation, a small outfit operating out of Levine's small studio in North Hollywood. Livingston didn't feel he was "getting the breaks" at Metro and decided it was better to be a big fish in a little pond than vice versa. "B" Westerns were very much in demand for the many theaters that regularly ran double features, and in the wake of Gene Autry's phenomenal success at Republic any actor who could warble a tune and stay in a saddle was a likely candidate for stardom.

Randall had the good fortune to be considered for a new series of musical Westerns being produced by Monogram, a pocket-size production and distribution entity run by W. Ray Johnston and Trem Carr. Founded in 1931, the company merged with Republic in 1935 but was reconstituted in 1937 following a series of disputes with president Herbert Yates. Johnston, Carr, and production chief Scott R. Dunlap intended to compete with Republic for the trade of independent exhibitors and small chains. Therefore, an Autry simulacrum was very much needed.

Jack Randall was no cowboy, but he looked acceptably virile in range togs and could at least hold a tune. He tested for the new Monogram Western series, was hired by Dunlap, and turned over to Robert North Bradbury, who had contracted to produce and direct the first three entries. With more than two decades of experience in directing Westerns, serials, and action-based melodramas, Bradbury—the father of second-tier cowboy star Bob Steele—knew all the tricks. In recent years he had helmed above-average oaters starring his son

Bob, John Wayne, and Johnny Mack Brown. He could be counted upon to whip the newly minted star into shape.

That would be no small task. Randall was a playboy who lived beyond his means and had a positive genius for getting himself into trouble with women. He drank heavily and was difficult to pin down. But he was canny enough to know when he was getting a break and therefore offered little resistance as Bradbury showed him the ropes.

Dunlap, a silent-era veteran who had guided the career of Buck Jones for many years before the coming of sound, knew the importance of investing extra money in the first installment of a new series. Studio sales departments worked hard to secure exhibitor commitments to blocks of films, including series Westerns released in groups of six or eight per year. Getting those commitments depended to a large extent on producing a strong opener that could be shown to theater owners and was representative of the entire series' quality. Exhibitors, like everybody else, relied on their initial impressions.

Randall's first vehicle was titled *Riders of the Dawn*. Based on an original story concocted by Bradbury and translated to scenario form by the prolific Robert Emmett Tansey, it was allotted a fairly generous budget. (Some sources say *Riders* cost $40,000, but that seems a little high for Monogram, which had spent as little as $10,000 just a few years earlier for its Lone Star releases starring John Wayne.) Dunlap okayed Bradbury's excursion to Lone Pine for location shooting and Bradbury's company went north in the late spring of 1937.

Randall got quick tutoring in horseback riding and six-gun handling, but Bradbury was taking no chances when action was concerned. Accompanying the unit to Lone Pine were three top stuntmen: Jack's principal double, Tom Steele, and Yakima Canutt and Cliff Lyons, who specialized in horse, wagon, and stagecoach stunts. Principal photography was completed in ten days. Bradbury shot the film's elaborate climactic chase on the "dry lake" slightly to the south and east of Lone Pine proper.

Riders of the Dawn begins with Randall, playing Marshal Jack Preston, riding and singing with his deputies. In the town of Mento, a grief-stricken man whose son has just been killed appeals to the townspeople for help. Grass Valley has been overrun

by outlaws headed by a ruthless criminal named Jim Danti, and the honest ranchers are terrified. Jack vows to bring to justice those responsible for the boy's death. He instructs his sidekick Grizzly (George Cooper) to be ready to ride at dawn, and orders his deputies to work "in the usual manner" and await his signal.

Danti (Warner Richmond) learns that a lawman is coming to Green Valley on a white horse. He arranges an ambush and one of his men accidentally shoots an outlaw named Tracy, who happens to be riding a horse matching the description of Jack's. The marshal, not far away, comes across Tracy, brings the mortally wounded man to a cabin nearby, and pins his badge on the outlaw after he dies. Jack reaches Grass Valley and poses as a badman named

Top: Randall the playboy, with first wife Barbara Bennett.
Bottom: Randall the Western star, in first publicity photo.

Two-Gun Gardner, recently released from jail. Danti is impressed with the newcomer's nerve and intelligence, agrees to an idea Jack cleverly proffers: that he pose as the new marshal.

Local Wells Fargo office manager Jean Porter (Peggy Keys) invites Jack to dinner. Later, as he serenades her, two of Danti's men overhear and tell their boss, who's had his eye on the girl. The instantly jealous outlaw chief is mollified when Jack explains that he used the dinner to persuade Jean to carry a large gold shipment on the next stage. In reality, the undercover lawman hopes he can capture Danti's men robbing the stage, giving him all the evidence he'll need to arrest them in one fell swoop.

The holdup goes awry and Jack is blamed by the townspeople for bungling the affair. Worse yet, the real Two-Gun Gardner arrives in town and tips Danti off to Jack's real identity. He also warns the bandit chieftain that Jack's deputies, whom he calls "white caps" for the bandanas they wear on their heads in battle, always turn up when the marshal is working undercover. Subsequently Two-Gun and Jack have a showdown, which the marshal wins. Believing the jig is nearly up, Danti precipitates a confrontation and has his men rob the bank. In the ensuing shootout Grizz is fatally shot trying to protect Jack.

The Danti gang flees into the desert, hotly pursued by the "white cap" deputies. A massive running gun battle rages as an electrical storm gets underway. Danti nearly escapes via stagecoach, but a bolt of lightning hits the coach, setting off a charge of dynamite. Jack and his deputies round up the surviving gang members and herd them off to the Mento jail—but not before the vindicated marshal tells Jean that he'll be back.

Released on July 14, 1937, *Riders of the Dawn* was generally well received, with some critics calling attention to the superbly executed action sequences. Randall himself got mixed notices, especially with regard to his singing. *Variety*'s review—probably the harshest the film received—said the tyro Western star "looks more like a musical comedy cowpuncher than a kiddie convincer." In typical *Variety* "slanguage" the paper's critic went on to lambaste the opening number: "Singing of star sounds oke but only with the eyes shut. Bad timing of sound makes the supposed singing from saddle ridiculously obvious to all but the blind."

Film historian Don Miller amplified this point in his 1976 chronicle of the "B" Western, *Hollywood Corral*: "[Randall] was victimized by inept recording, photographed in close-up bobbing up and down in the saddle as he went through his number without a quiver or a quaver. It was so patently phony that even the smaller fry weren't fooled for a moment. Randall never managed to recover from this unimpressive musical beginning, and his other songs were greeted with audible squirming from the audience, thus taking the edge off a superior Western."

For the fan of Lone Pine in movies, the high point of *Riders of the Dawn* is undoubtedly its action-packed last reel, excitingly staged by director Bradbury and expertly photographed by Bert Longenecker, who served as cinematographer on all but a few of Randall's starring Westerns. Another prominent

historian, William K. Everson, described the film's stirring finale in his 1992 book *The Hollywood Western*:

It is a running battle between a posse of lawmen and the villains, some of whom are in a stagecoach. The effectiveness of the climax was increased by a reshaping of the Hopalong Cassidy formula, a slow and methodical buildup in which background music was suddenly introduced to underline the action. But in this instance the climax itself was subjected to a repetition of that formula: a street gun duel, the hero riding off to collect his waiting posses, the baddies' bank holdup and escape, this *then* merging into the pitched running battle. This final chase, staged on salt flats and with much unusual angling in the camerawork, would have done credit to a much larger production. Since the location appears to have been

Jack Randall comforts the victim of a holdup in *Riders of the Dawn* (1937), his first starring Western.

at least partially the same, and Yakima Canutt performs similar stunt work in both films, one must assume that somehow the sequence came to John Ford's attention, for its similarities to his salt flats chase in *Stagecoach* are unmistakable.

Riders of the Dawn impressed exhibitors enough to take a chance on the entire 1937-38 group of Randall Westerns, but as the star never posed a serious threat to such warbling waddies as Gene Autry, Tex Ritter, or Dick Foran, the musical numbers were dropped after the first few series entries. And from what we can tell, nobody complained about that.

Bradbury completed his three-picture commitment and Randall's fortunes were entrusted next to producer Maurice Conn, who had just finished a Western series starring Kermit Maynard. An old hand at turning out quality "B"-grade pictures on quick schedules for short money, Conn worked well with Randall, who was difficult to handle. The star was openly contemptuous of his Westerns and, according to some of his co-workers, refused to take his work seriously. A careless actor, he frequently forgot his lines and missed his marks, necessitating more retakes than usual in such productions. Worse yet, he had a tendency to rush through his lines and

Randall intervenes in an ambush by Warner Richmond in this scene from *Riders of the Dawn*.

often got tongue-tied, tripping over his own words. He also seemed to have trouble controlling his horse, but skillful doubling in chase sequences maintained the illusion that he was an expert rider.

For the last entry in the 1937-38 "season," Conn hired director Robert F. Hill, who had long been an advocate of shooting in Lone Pine's Alabama Hills as a means of imparting production value to parsimoniously produced horse operas. Hill was fortunate in that *Man's Country* gave him a superior Robert Tansey script from which to work, and that Conn secured an excellent cast of supporting players.

The story begins with sinister rancher Lex Crane (Walter Long) surrendering his son Ted (David Sharpe) to local peace officers after the young man is accused of a murder he did not commit. While the lawmen are taking the boy to town, though, Ted is shot and killed from ambush by Bert (Dave O'Brien), a henchman of Buck Crane, Lex's twin brother. When the section is subsequently terrorized by outlaws, the local citizens conclude that Lex and his men are behind the depredations.

Ranger Jack Hale (Randall) and his sidekick Snappy (Ralph Peters) are assigned to apprehend Lex, who by now has become accustomed to being considered a renegade. They join the Crane outfit with the unwitting aid of Lex's daughter Madge (Marjorie Reynolds), and after a short time Jack learns that Ted was murdered because of something he found in the underground caves on his father's property. When Lex tells Jack that his brother Buck covets the ranch, the undercover ranger begins to think that the errant brother is actually behind the crimes for which Lex has been blamed.

Unfortunately, before securing the evidence he needs, Jack is exposed as a ranger and threatened with death at the hands of Lex's loyal cowboys. But the rancher will have none of this and surrenders to Jack for his own good. Eventually Hale learns that Buck is hoping Lex will be executed for the crimes he committed, because then he'll inherit the ranch and what's beneath it—a fortune in oil deposits.

Jack is kidnapped by Buck's men and tells the outlaw that proof of his crimes is at the ranger's station, for which the gang departs immediately, carrying enough dynamite to blow the place to smithereens and destroy the evidence. After escaping, Jack races

ordinary turns and seldom drags." Other reviewers singled out the fine work of Walter Long as twin brothers and Marjorie Reynolds in the normally nominal ingénue role.

Randall's final Lone Pine outing was one of his best Westerns—and also one of the cheapest. Robert Tansey had been promoted to producer and tasked with bringing in his films for less money than had been allotted to earlier entries in the series. He wrote a script without scenes requiring interiors, thereby avoiding the need for studio rental and set construction. It was hardly a new or novel practice, but one that could easily be utilized when shooting in Lone Pine: With the majestic Sierra Nevadas as a backdrop for the story, who needed cramped sound-stage sets?

The film went into production as *Riders of the Rio Grande*. Principal photography began in Lone Pine in mid-February of 1939, with snow still readily apparent on the Sierra mountaintops, lending a fillip to the cinematography of Bert Longenecker and Henry Freulich. Director Spencer Gordon Bennett, like Bob Hill an old hand at cranking out "B" Westerns on shoestring budgets, proved unusually adaptable to the demand of a Jack Randall picture shot on location. Later he recalled making movies in Lone Pine with words almost identical to those uttered by other directors in later years: "The great thing about Lone Pine is that you can put your camera down in one spot and get four or five different setups just by aiming your camera in different directions and moving your reflectors to catch the sun wherever it is in the sky."

The completed picture, retitled *Across the Plains*, made use of a familiar if not downright clichéd plot.

When their wagon train is attacked by outlaws and their parents killed, young brother Jimmy and Jack

to the station and, with the help of newly deputized Lex and his ranch hands, apprehends Buck and his gang. Lex's name is clear, freeing Jack and Madge to develop their burgeoning relationship.

Like most Hill-directed Westerns shot at Lone Pine, *Man's Country* made good use of the Alabama Hills, which looked particularly impressive as a result of Bert Longenecker's careful camera placements. *Variety*, never overly fond of Randall's efforts, admitted that the picture "possesses more believable intrigue and suspense than is often found in these outdoor operas.... Yarn has a couple of out-of-the-

Jack Randall and leading lady Marjorie Reynolds pose prettily in the Alabama Hills for this photo from *Man's Country* (1938).

Winters, two young brothers, are separated. Jimmy is taken by the renegades, while Jack is adopted by a band of roving Indians. Years later, a wagon master named Buckskin (Hal Price) meets Jack (Randall), who goes by the name of Cherokee. The two men join forces, helping pioneers whenever they can but always hoping to avenge the murder of Jack's parents. They're joined by Cherokee's Mexican pal, Lopez Mendoza (Frank Yaconelli).

Jimmy has grown up to become the Kansas Kid (Dennis Moore), right-hand man of aging desperado Buff Gordon (Bob Card). Kansas has taken a job as guide to a wagon train headed by Jeff Masters (Glenn Strange), who is accompanied by his daughter Mary (Joyce Bryant). The Kid plans on leading the Masters outfit into an ambush at Rainbow Canyon. Cherokee happens on the wagon train and diverts it to the town of Wagon Springs, where Masters plans to establish a freight line. Kansas is forced to acquiesce lest he be exposed as an outlaw. He has no idea that Cherokee is his long-lost brother.

Later, the gang concocts a plan to rob a gold shipment of gold and decides to eliminate Cherokee before he can interfere with them again. They capture Buckskin, hoping to lure Cherokee into a trap. The grizzled old rider overhears Buff remind one of his men that the Kid still doesn't know they killed his parents. Learning about Buckskin's plight, Cherokee storms the outlaw camp to rescue Buckskin and have a showdown with Kansas. The old timer springs the news that they are brothers. The Kid, who has always believed Indians killed his parents, learns that Buff was the real murderer. As some gang members attack Masters' freight wagons, the brothers team up to wipe out Buff and the others. In the gun battle that follows, the Kid is mortally wounded but meets

Randall as "Cherokee," hero of *Across the Plains* (1939), in a makeshift corral in the Alabama Hills.

death with the knowledge that his parents have been avenged.

Released that June, *Across the Plains* found a receptive audience among action-hungry Western fans. Bennet's unobtrusive direction stressed rapid movement and exploited the Alabama Hills quite effectively. His talent for making less seem like more was demonstrated in a sequence unfolding at a settlement where Jeff Masters planned to open his business. By carefully grouping wagons, props, and extras—and then having cinematographer Longenecker shoot it fairly close up—Bennet created the illusion of a busy settlement that wasn't really there. This type of deception was, by necessity, carried out frequently by filmmakers specializing in low-budget product. The Bob Bradburys, Bob Hills, and Spencer Bennets were better at it than most, which is why they had little trouble finding employment even in the dark Depression days of the Thirties.

From *Across the Plains*: Cherokee's adopted family in the Hills with the Sierras making a beautiful background.

Randall with frequent sidekick Frank Yaconelli.
Below: Randall tangles with Warner Richmond again.

Unfortunately, the above-average nature of *Riders of the Dawn*, *Man's Country*, and *Across the Plains* was not enough to keep Jack Randall afloat in a veritable sea of cowboy stars, singing and otherwise. He was already starting to sink when Monogram consigned his movies to ultra-cheapo producer Harry S. Webb, whose 1939-40 Randall entries were hamstrung with weak (some might say non-existent) stories and slipshod technical work. Entrusting the foundering star to Webb was like tossing him an anchor. He sank like a stone, losing his berth at Monogram and his stardom as well. Randall changed his name to Allen Byron and won supporting roles in several mid-Forties programmers. His final appearance before a motion-picture camera was never seen by his erstwhile fans: Randall died in 1945 while playing a heavy in a Universal serial titled *The Royal Mounted Rides Again*. He was shooting a chase scene when his horse veered off the trail and slammed him into a tree. It was a sad finish to a career that once held promise. ☐☐☐

TRIGGER TOM
AND HIS LADY MARION

This attractive screen team made two enjoyable "B" Westerns in Lone Pine.

by Richard W. Bann

The two 1936 films made in Lone Pine with "B"-Western and serial star Tom Tyler—*Rip Roarin' Buckaroo* and *Phantom of the Range*—both featured Beth Marion. They, like her, are now only footnotes in film history that remain worthy of closer attention. Neither film, and neither star, is mentioned anywhere in Dave Holland's trail-blazing book on moviemaking in the area, *On Location in Lone Pine*. Nor, for that matter, is the director of both films, the long-forgotten Robert F. (Bob) Hill—who, like his one-time associate Clarence Badger, was an early advocate of filmmaking in Lone Pine.

Ruggedly handsome, muscular Tom Tyler was born Vincent Markowski near Albany, New York. His parents moved to Hamtramck, a suburb of Detroit, when the boy was ten. There he attended Catholic schools and dreamed of breaking into movies. He left home at 16 despite his parents' objections. On his way west to Hollywood the young film aspirant worked

as a lumberjack, coal miner, and prizefighter—this last presaging his character in *Rip Roarin' Buckaroo*.

Tyler landed bit roles in cheap features and serials before becoming a top-billed star in *Let's Go Gallagher* (1925), the first in a Western series produced initially by Robertson-Cole Pictures and distributed by Film Booking Offices, Inc. These sturdily made independent oaters teamed the tall, brawny Tyler with diminutive Frankie Darro, an accomplished and athletic child star.

Tom bridged the gap between silent and sound movies with a series released by Trem Carr's Syndicate Pictures, forerunner of Monogram Pictures. He was intimidated by the advent of talkies because his voice recorded poorly, but he worked steadily for a number of Poverty Row producers. Tyler had a lengthy run with Reliable Pictures Corporation, an indie outfit run by Harry S. Webb and Bernard B. Ray, shoestring producers who specialized in "B" pictures shot fast and cheap. When his Western series was canceled, Tom signed with Sam Katzman's newly formed Victory Pictures Corporation. Having learned the picture business as a production manager and supervisor for independent producer A. W. Hackel, Katzman launched his own production unit in 1936. *Rip Roarin' Buckaroo* was to be the first of eight Victory Westerns starring Tyler.

Beth Marion was horn on July 11, 1912 in Clinton, Iowa. She studied speech at Northwestern University in Evanston. Illinois. Because of her striking looks and sex appeal she was pulled into local stage productions. This work led to her engagement as a singer with the Paul Whiteman Orchestra in 1931. Hoping to break into movies, she went to California at age 22. She hoped to get into comedy and before making any Westerns won a small role in the 1935 Hal Roach two-reel short subject, *Twin Triplets*, starring Thelma Todd and Patsy Kelly.

Beth's agent found it easier to arrange employment in outdoor action shows than in slapstick or screwball comedies, which she preferred. She met the two principal qualifications for employment as a heroine in low-budget series Westerns: she could rivet attention effectively while mounting and dismounting a horse, and she was pretty. More than pretty: She was beautiful. And more than beautiful, she was sexy. Consequently, she made movies opposite Western stars Buck Jones, Bob Steele, Ken Maynard, his brother Kermit, Johnny Mack Brown, Jack Luden, and George Houston. By the time Katzman hired her for the two Tyler pictures, she had already worked in Lone Pine several times, most notably in *Between Men* (1935), the first Johnny Mack Brown Western produced under the auspices of Katzman's former employer, A. W. Hackel. At this time Beth was married to Cliff

Lyons, a minor-league star of silent horse operas now working most frequently as a stunt double.

Early in September 1936 *The Hollywood Reporter* noted that the first of Victory's Tyler westerns, *Rip Roarin' Buckaroo*, would start shooting the following Tuesday. In fact, the plan called for making two pictures, pretty much simultaneously, with nearly identical casts and at the same location: Lone Pine. Low-budget producers achieved great economics of scale with this production method of doubling up on location excursions.

Tom Tyler (wearing fedora) accompanied by Sammy Cohen in this scene from *Rip Roarin' Buckaroo* (1936).

Unsung "B"-film director Bob Hill knew that Lone Pine was a dramatic, extremely pictorial locale that would automatically give his work an important look and help launch the Tyler series with some class and momentum. Hill knew well that by shooting in Lone Pine he could accrue tremendous production value for the Tylers at no incremental cost, except for those associated with the requisite travel. Lone Pine was pretty much the farthest that producers went outside Hollywood to shoot on location, within the state of California.

On Monday, September 7, the Tyler company packed up and drove some 250 miles north to Lone Pine in order to be ready to turn cameras on the first filmed action, Tuesday morning at sunrise. The Tyler company actively shot the pictures "two up" (at the same time), from sunrise till sundown. Back at the Dow Hotel every evening there was time only for dinner, drinks, and memorizing lines in the script for the next day's scenes. In all likelihood, "rushes" of the day's work were screened at Pearson's, the local movie house.

Rip Roarin' Buckaroo tells the tale of prizefighter Scotty McWade (Tyler), the loser of a fixed bout. Disgusted by the fight racket, he retires, conceals his boxing identity, and is hired as a ranch hand. When he mounts and masters a seemingly unrideable horse, the rancher, called "the Colonel" (John Elliott), gives the mare to McWade and asks him to represent the ranch in a race. Then the same crooked fight promoter (Forrest Taylor) arrives and wagers heavily on the outcome with the Colonel.

McWade tries to warn the beleaguered rancher and his daughter. Betty Rose (Beth Marion), but is rebuffed. She slaps Scotty for his impertinence. So he departs and rides off into the rocks (where Tyler proves why he wasn't a singing cowboy with his a cappella rendition of "Home on the Range"). Upon learning her father has gambled the ranch, Betty Rose finds McWade and pleads with him to return and enter the horse race. He does, he wins, and after a series of charges and frame-ups (in which McWade is jailed) there is another match in the squared arena, more wagering, and this time

Cohen pointing something out to Tyler, with Lone Pine landmark Rattlesnake Mountain in the background.

Scotty smashes his way to the Pacific Coast light-heavyweight title he was cheated out of before. The two-fisted battler retires a second time, and happily kisses Betty Rose.

As *Phantom of the Range* begins, a miserly old rancher has died, ostensibly deep in debt. Crooks, however, led by a neighbor (Taylor), believe a treasure of riches is hidden somewhere on the dead man's property. They create a myth that the rancher still rides the range as a ghost—the phantom—hoping to scare off prospective buyers until these thieves can go digging and locate his fortune. During an auction to liquidate the property and its assets, Jerry Lane (Tyler) arrives hoping to acquire just such a ranch as his new home. So does the old man's granddaughter, Jeanne Moore (Marion). She has traveled there to press her inheritance claim on the homestead, but is without sufficient funds to discharge the debts against it.

With folding money bulging in his pockets, Lane outbids the crooks and Miss Moore both, but he's smitten with her and hires the beautiful young lady as a secretary. He also retains a cockney kleptomaniac (Sammy Cohen) as his valet. In due course Lane finds a map hidden in a picture frame, leading him to the treasure's location, secreted at a place called Tower Rocks. Inexplicably, the riches can only be unearthed beneath a full moon. Which they are, in a whirlwind climax. But who can claim the treasure? Lane? Or Moore? The valet reminds the pair. "I thought you were going to pool your resources." Lane smiles, looks at Miss Moore, and asks. "Well?" She answers, as music for the fade-out is turned up, " 'Well' yourself, fella!"

On Saturday, September 19, *The Hollywood Reporter* carried this story: "Sam Katzman's Western troupe will return Monday from Lone Pine, where it has been on location shooting scenes for two Tom

Top: Tyler's first bronc-riding effort doesn't end so well. Veteran Western player Charles King stands next to Cohen.
Bottom: Now in full cowboy-star regalia, Tom gets serious with Beth Marion in *Rip Roarin' Buckaroo*.

Beth Marion is driving Forrest Taylor to town when they meet Tom Tyler in the Alabama Hills.

Tyler films. *Rip Roarin' Buckaroo* and *Phantom of' the Range,* Beth Marion is leading lady."

On that Monday, the same publication printed its regular production summary chart, which indicated the Tyler unit had devoted eight shooting days to the two pictures while in Lone Pine. Upon returning to Culver City, interiors were lensed at the Victory studio. In the interim someone screening the rushes for the first time made the point that amply endowed Beth Marion ought to be wearing a brassiere! Consequently, footage in either film showing her passing from indoors (on a Culver City soundstage) to outdoors (in Lone Pine) does not match, for two unmistakable reasons.

Yiddish comedian Cohen appeared in both Lone Pine Tylers, as did most of the other supporting actors, a collection of low-paid favorites from outdoor action-adventure pictures: John Elliott, Dick Cramer, the ubiquitous Charlie King (alleged to have studied medicine for two years at Southwestern University, according to Victory publicity), and Forrest Taylor. Elliott and Taylor must have been friends of director Hill, since both were frequently cast in his pictures.

The white-haired director often appeared in films he helmed. In *Rip Roarin' Buckaroo* he officiates at the horse race. This happens to he quite an interesting scene, shot in the town of Lone Pine itself. The horses line up for the race, facing north, at the intersection of Jackson and Bush Streets, The camera setup appears to be approximately where the sidewalk is today in front of Statham Hall, the dealers' room at the Festival, and former site of Pearson's theater— where Hill's unit probably screened dailies for both these films! The race itself is run throughout what

Tom Tyler is about to spring into action, but Sammy Cohen doesn't seem to be taking matters seriously.

were then dirt roads on the east side of town, all familiar today to anyone who has glanced around Lone Pine.

In addition to the magnificent landscape scenery captured among the rugged Alabama Hills, both Tyler pictures are distinguished by views they offer inside the town as it looked in 1936. Nearly all films shot in Lone Pine trek up instead toward the eastern slope of the white granite Sierra mountains before any cameras turn: They almost never show the hamlet stretching but a few blocks at the base of Mount Whitney with shops and residences. Both *Rip Roarin' Buckaroo* and *Phantom of the Range* provide glimpses of the same streets and stores Lone Pine Film Festival attendees see all day. Both have been run in the past at the Festival, eliciting audible surprise from Lone Pine residents in the audience.

In correspondence with the author during 1983 and 1984, Beth Marion wrote, "I had a lot of fun and pleasure doing the two Westerns with Tom Tyler, a very handsome and nice fellow. We made them at the same time up north in Lone Pine. California. Gosh, they were quickies.

"I also rode back from location with Tom Tyler after our two Lone Pine Westerns. We really got to know each other and shared some confidential things…. He was going to marry little Jeanne Martel and was deeply in love with her. He was quiet and shy and so nice…. His parents were from Lithuania, and he had to speak so carefully that he over-

pronounced words so as not to betray any kind of accent. He worked hard on that. He told me a voice coach gave him lessons when talking pictures came into vogue."

We have plenty of reasons to be grateful to Bob Hill, responsible for bringing so many film crews to Lone Pine, but he was not a skilled or sensitive director. There is little subtlety in his work, and it's obvious that on his sets, the acting talent received little help. John Elliott and Forrest Taylor were capable senior performers, but others in these films are guilty of acting's cardinal sin: "indicating." It's clear Beth Marion is overacting in scenes where she tries to get across certain emotions. And Tyler, too, is straining to be casual and likable. His evident discomfort at this makes us uneasy as well, because the camera does not lie.

Rip Roarin' Buckaroo was quickly made available to theaters, carrying a national release date of October 15, 1936, while domestic issuance of *Phantom of the Range* followed on November 28. Gross revenues ranged from $50,000 to $60,000 per picture. For

Tyler comforts a mortally wounded man in this dramatic scene from *Phantom of the Range* (1936).

Director Bob Hill (with starter pistol) in this horse-race sequence shot in the streets of Lone Pine.

Tyler publicly pummels a heavy on a Lone Pine street in this scene from *Phantom of the Range*.

POR. 46

Beth Marion is accosted by a tough customer who apparently doesn't realize Tyler is about to smack him.

comparison, the following year's *Hollywood Cowboy* (1937), starring George O'Brien and partially shot in Lone Pine, generated worldwide film rentals of $223.000.

Tom Tyler made six more pictures to fulfill his contract with Victory. Two co-starred his new wife, Jeanne Martel. Like many heroes of the cinematic range, Tyler turned to personal appearances, touring for a season with the Wallace Bros. Circus. Unlike most of his action-hero contemporaries, Tyler would play heavies, or character bits, in grade-"A" movies: Most agree he made a better villain in big pictures than he did a hero in programmers. Examples include *Stagecoach* (1939), *Gone With the Wind* (1939), *The Grapes of Wrath* (1940), *The Westerner* (1940), *Talk of the Town* (1942), and *Red River* (1948). In 1941 he began a two-year stint in Republic's Three Mesquiteers series, his last as a cowboy star. That year he returned as the star of *Adventures of Captain Marvel*. In a 1943 chapter play, his last, Tyler played another comic-strip hero: *The Phantom*. And he was

a worthy bandaged successor to Boris Karloff as the disfigured Kharis, titular terror of *The Mummy's Hand (1940)*.

Eventually Tyler saw his masterful physique ravaged and atrophied by rheumatoid arthritis, and injuries sustained in a serious car accident altered his facial features. By the early Fifties he had been reduced to tiny, unsympathetic roles, pretty much unrecognizable and virtually penniless. Returning to Hamtramck in November 1952, Tyler moved in with his sister, abandoned his screen name, and labored as a factory worker when his condition permitted. He suffered a fatal heart attack, dying at age 50 on May 1, 1954. "I was shocked when I heard he died," wrote Beth Marion years later. "Cliff told me. I didn't see how it was possible because he was such a muscular fellow and seemed invincible!"

To placate Cliff Lyons, Beth Marion left movies in 1938 to raise their two sons. In a letter written 30 years ago, she explained that after marrying Lyons, she felt pressure from him to retire from movies. "He

Forrest Taylor thinks he's about to get the drop on Tom Tyler in this tense scene from *Phantom of the Range*. Frankly, we don't think that's going to happen.

Roundup time in the Alabama Hills. Tyler has the situation—along with Forrest Taylor and Charlie King—well in hand. Notice Rattlesnake Mountain in the background.

was an extremely jealous sort of man," Beth wrote, "so I would travel with him on location to places like Lone Pine and Kernville." After divorcing Lyons in 1955, she tried resuming her film career, appearing in TV commercials, industrial films, and two 1955 features, *Ain't Misbehavin'* and *A Man Called Peter*. Her second marriage, to architect Julian Koch, was

happier. In retirement she painted for fun and lived in a beautiful mobile home in Jacksonville, Oregon. She displayed her work before amazed fans at two film festivals she attended years later. Beth passed away at age 90 on February 18, 2003. Her younger half-brother is George Paul, long time producer-director on the ABC-TV series *20/20*. □□□

Hoppy and Billy, the Bar 20 Boys

How a 12-year-old trick rider got to meet and work with one of his movie idols.

by Ed Hulse

No cowboy star is more closely identified with Lone Pine than William Boyd. Fully half of his 66 "Hopalong Cassidy" Westerns boasted sequences filmed in the Alabama Hills and the adjacent area, and many Hoppys were shot entirely in Lone Pine.

Producer Harry "Pop" Sherman knew that the picturesque Sierra Nevada mountains and the rugged high-desert terrain made terrific backdrops for the Cassidy films, which started out a cut above most "B" Westerns and maintained high standards during his nine-year stewardship.

Billy King

From the beginning Boyd's starring vehicles trounced the competition. They may have lacked the plentiful, indiscriminate action of some horse operas, but their scripts were a notch better than the average and their production values—thanks in large measure to the Lone Pine locations—made them standouts in their class of Western. Having his pictures released by Paramount, which owned its own theater chain and therefore guaranteed playdates in prestigious downtown movie palaces, compelled Pop Sherman to provide a level of quality other "B"-Western producers rarely attained and seldom even aspired to.

Sherman produced the Cassidy Westerns in groups of six. The first-season entries (1935-36) were helmed by Howard Bretherton, a long-time assistant director just beginning to make his own mark when Pop hired him. The second six (1936-37) were directed by another veteran "a.d." named Nate Watt, whose credits as assistant included *All Quiet on the Western Front.* Sherman had financed the initial sextet independently, but Paramount put up money for the second-year offerings. The Hoppys had become far more successful than the studio anticipated, so it was in Paramount's interest to boost the budgets and provide Pop with additional resources. The six 1936-37 series entries were slightly more extravagant and had longer running times to justify occasional playdates at the top of double bills.

For the third group, scheduled for release during the 1937-38 "season," Harry Sherman engaged as unit director one Lesley Selander, who had recently directed Buck Jones Westerns for Universal. That studio's abrupt termination of the Jones series left Selander jobless, and it is believed that Buck himself—a friend of Bill Boyd—recommended the young helmer to Boyd and/or Sherman.

Other changes were in the offing. For example, the first 12 Hoppys had used background music sparingly, usually just for the last-reel action windup, featuring *agitato* and *furioso* cues rented from the Meyer

Synchronization Service, which catered primarily to Poverty Row producers. Abe Meyer's music was perfectly adequate, but Paramount believed the Hopalong Cassidy pictures deserved better. So, beginning with the 1937-38 releases, Sherman's films were scored with cues written for such major Paramount productions as *The Plainsman*, *The Texas Rangers*, and *Trail of the Lonesome Pine*.

Also, after shooting the eleventh and twelfth Hoppys on a trial basis, Russell Harlan was promoted to unit cinematographer. He had started with Paramount in the electrical department, handling with soundstage lights, and worked himself up to assistant cameraman. Harlan knew his way around a light meter and was also proficient in the use of filters, which were frequently employed on outdoor pictures to create such effects as "day for night." His association with Pop Sherman lasted ten years; subsequently he was director of photography on such classics as *Red Rider* (1948), *The Thing from Another World* (1951), *Witness for the Prosecution* (1957), and *To Kill a Mockingbird* (1962). His contribution to the Hopalong Cassidy series—and especially those installments shot at Lone Pine—is almost inestimable.

The first two groups of Hoppy Westerns had established a winning formula. While not strictly adhering to the Cassidy novels written by Clarence E. Mulford, they took place in a West not entirely unrecognizable to fans of the author's stories. The mighty Bar-20 ranch, managed (and later owned) by Buck Peters, was a sort of Camelot, with Buck functioning more or less as a cactus King Arthur, with Hopalong as his Galahad, and the other hands as his Knights of the Round Table. In the aggregate they were, as Cassidy himself once described the Bar 20 boys, "a pretty salty bunch,"

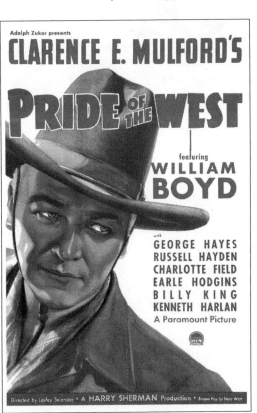

but they were also fiercely loyal to each other and confident in their belief system: The law was all right as far as it went, but justice could be obtained by other means when necessary.

Mulford's Hopalong was a red-haired, tobacco-chewing, profanity-spewing puncher whose closest friends were Red Connors and Johnny Nelson. Hollywood's Hopalong was slightly more genteel, and his saddle pals were impetuous Johnny Nelson and grizzled old-timer Windy Halliday. The latter was an invention of screenwriter Doris Schroeder, who introduced him in *Bar 20 Rides Again* (1935), a loose adaptation of one of Mulford's best yarns. Red had appeared in the first film, *Hop-a-long Cassidy* (also 1935) but, curiously, was dropped in later entries. James Ellison essayed the role of Johnny Nelson until 1937, when he left the series after playing Buffalo Bill Cody in Cecil B. De Mille's big-budget Western *The Plainsman*. The character of Johnny Nelson was mothballed temporarily, and *Hills of Old Wyoming* (1937) introduced Russell Hayden as Lucky Jenkins, presumably based on Mesquite Jenkins, whom Mulford had introduced in a 1923 series of short stories published in book form as *Hopalong Cassidy Returns*. Unwilling to rock the boat, Sherman's scripters cast Lucky in the same mold as Johnny; like the earlier youthful protégé, he was portrayed as headstrong, impetuous, and chronically lovesick. Windy was played by venerable character actor George Hayes, for this writer's money the best sidekick ever to appear in "B" Westerns. The role of Buck Peters had been taken in the first film by Charles Middleton, better known as a heavy, but beginning with *Three on the Trail* (1936) he was played by William Duncan, a silent-screen leading man whose Westerns and serials for Vitagraph had made him a star in the Teens and early Twenties.

Left to Right: George Hayes, William Boyd, Billy King, William Duncan, Russell Hayden, and Lois Wilde in *Hopalong Rides Again* (1937), Billy's first film and one of the series' best.

Today, Billy King is a sprightly, talkative 88-year-old gentleman who enthusiastically recalled his brief tenure with the Hopalong Cassidy unit for *Lone Pine in the Movies*. "They were looking for a kid to add to the cast," Billy told us. "Somebody, a casting director or something like that, touted me to Pop Sherman, who called me down to Hollywood. They knew about my riding and the competitions I'd won. Pop interviewed and signed me up for a weekly salary. It was pretty exciting to a kid like me."

At the time, King and his friends were avid fans of the Hopalong Cassidy films. "Oh, my God!" he exclaimed. "He was my hero! We used to see his movies in the Saturday matinees, you know. We were crazy for them. Pretending to shoot up the theater, and all that. It's difficult to explain to people today what a big deal those pictures were back then."

Going into its third year the series now had its best quartet of principal players: Boyd, Hayden, Hayes, and Duncan. That's the combination revered by most devotees of the Hopalong Cassidy movies.

An addition to the regular cast had a significant impact on the 1937-38 Hoppy films. Since the series had proven popular with the adolescent boys who largely populated Saturday-matinee screenings, it was believed that adding to the movies a lad from that age group would give youthful viewers someone with whom to identify. As it happened, the new hire was himself a huge fan of Hopalong Cassidy.

In 1937 Billy King was 12 years old. Born and reared in Northern California, he was the son of a professional horse trainer and as a result was used to the saddle at an age when most other kids are just learning how to ride bicycles. Billy's dad bought the boy's first horse, a year-old mustang named Tony after Tom Mix's famous steed, and together they trained and eventually competed for prizes in rodeos at county and state fairs. By the time he turned 12 the youngster had already won more than two dozen ribbons, a fact Paramount highlighted in publicity materials.

After signing his one-year, four-picture contract with Harry Sherman, Billy was introduced to his idol, William Boyd, and director Lesley Selander. He still remembers Boyd flashing that famous grin, extending his hand, and saying, "Hello, Billy. It's a pleasure to be working with you and your horse."

Boyd had just married his fifth wife, actress Grace Bradley, who would have an enormously positive impact on the actor, whose personal life had previously been, to put it politely, rather eventful. After two years in the role that would dominate the rest of his life, Boyd was just beginning to realize that, like it or not, he was a role model for children—a responsibility he took seriously. "I believe it was around this time he bought the idea that he could be a hero for kids," King recalled. "But he had to 'sell' that idea to Pop Sherman. I don't think Pop was entirely on board with it at first. That's where I came in."

Several sources, beginning with Jon Tuska's

fascinating but flawed 1976 history of horse operas, *The Filming of the West*, have stated that Boyd hated children and resented that his popularity depended on their approbation. King categorically denies this. "That's an absolute lie," he stated firmly when we asked about it. "No truth to it whatsoever. I knew the man, I worked alongside him. He couldn't have been nicer to me. But I also know how strongly he felt about the effect his pictures had on kids. This was not a man who hated kids."

With King added to the cast of the season's first entry, already announced as *Hopalong Rides Again*, it remained only to make a place for him in the story.

Windy Halliday (Hayes) teaches Artie Peters (King) the finer points of gun twirling in this scene from *Hopalong Rides Again*.

Another newcomer to the Hopalong Cassidy unit was screenwriter Norman Houston, who supplanted Doris Schroeder and Harrison Jacobs as the series' primary scripters. For his first assignment Houston was given a Mulford novel to adapt. It was *Black Buttes,* a 1923 page-turner but not a Cassidy yarn. That hardly mattered, because Houston didn't adapt the original story any more closely than previous screenwriters employed by Sherman. In fact, from the Mulford tale Houston took only the location of the rustlers' stomping grounds—the Black Buttes— and the name of the villain, Hepburn. The rest of the story was cut to the series' familiar pattern, with one or two important exceptions.

The first was Hopalong's mild flirtation with leading lady Nora Lane, cast as Hepburn's widowed sister. Although Cassidy had previously tickled the fancies of female characters (specifically, Evelyn Brent in *Hopalong Cassidy Returns* and Bernadine Hayes in *North of the Rio Grande*), he had never instigated a romance. But Houston's screenplay gave him a potential paramour for the first time. Pretty rancher Nora Blake had one drawback, though: her brother, Horace Hepburn. Ostensibly a professor of paleontology, he was actually secret chief of the rustler band that camped out in the forbidding Black Buttes and preyed upon cattlemen forced to drive their herds through that benighted area.

The second exception to the previously established formula was the introduction of young Archibald Peters—Artie, for short—the nephew of Bar 20 owner Buck Peters. Artie was a bit of a pest, an Eastern lad spending summer vacation on his uncle's sprawling spread and getting underfoot. The Bar 20 hands, especially Windy, often feigned exasperation when he was around, but secretly they were all fond of him.

Houston's adaptation kicks into high gear when Artie persuades Buck to let him join Hopalong on a potentially dangerous cattle drive through the Black Buttes, everybody fears he will be a nuisance. Those fears are realized when Hepburn's men dynamite the buttes and send a rockslide crashing down on the chuck wagon in which Artie is riding with Windy. The boy's injuries force Windy to stay with him while Hopalong sets out to trap the rustlers. But Artie plays a pivotal role in the story's climax by courageously riding back to the Bar 20

Windy and Artie take cover under the chuck wagon to avoid a dynamite-induced rockslide in *Hopalong Rides Again*.

in a weakened state and leading Buck and the boys to the spot where the cattle thieves plan to ambush Hoppy and Lucky. (As scripted, the last-reel sequence would give Billy King ample opportunity to demonstrate his considerable riding ability. He rode his own horse, Tony, in this and his other Hopalong Cassidy movies.)

Principal photography got underway in early June of 1937, shortly after Boyd's marriage to Grace Bradley. Still honeymooning, the couple arranged to live in the log cabin on Lone Pine's Tuttle Creek Road during the production period. The other cast and crew members bunked in town, most of them at the Dow Villa Hotel, which still stands and has recently been restored to resemble its 1930s look.

Billy King was fascinated by the entire production process. "I had no idea, no appreciation for the logistics that are involved in making a movie out in the Alabama Hills," he said recently. "It's a very complicated thing, you know—moving all the cameras and equipment, the horses and cattle, getting everybody on location, feeding them, choosing the camera setups. To me Pop Sherman was a genius. He really showed a lot of people in Hollywood how to do things, you know, on a budget, and still wind up with a quality picture."

The film was called *Texas Trail*, but Billy King went with Boyd, Hayden, and Hayes to Arizona for location shooting.

Much has been written on, and many previous Film Festival guests have spoken to, the arduousness of working in and around Lone Pine. As a 12-year-old boy, Billy King didn't find the work physically taxing or potentially dangerous. "Everybody was very cautious," he says today. "The hours were long but, you know, there was always food and water and what not. Those people were used to this sort of thing; they had everything well worked out by the time I came along. But it was a complicated process, for sure."

Some 65 years after it was made, what distinguishes *Hopalong Rides Again*—in addition to the sturdiness of its deceptively simple plot, the romantic byplay between Boyd and Lane, and the smoothness of Selander's directorial style—is its use of the Alabama Hills, where the majority of the action takes place, and of that little house on Tuttle Creek Road now and forevermore known as "the Hoppy cabin." There are scenes in *Hopalong Rides Again* that show

certain outcroppings this writer has never seen in any other Lone Pine movie. The case could be made that the 13th Hoppy has the best scenic shots of the whole series, although an equally strong case could be made for Selander's third Cassidy film, *Heart of Arizona* (1938), which also featured Billy King and is discussed below. Standing in for the menacing Black Buttes, the Hills are practically characters in their own right. Those Buttes, soaked with the blood of cattlemen ambushed by merciless rustlers who afterward conceal themselves with near-supernatural ease, are spoken of with reverential awe and barely disguised foreboding.

For someone who had worked in Lone Pine only once before (on the 1937 Buck Jones film *Sandflow*), Selander showed an amazing affinity for the area's visual allure. With the help of cinematographer Harlan, the new director captured many breathtaking shots of the Sierra foothills. His staging of scenes always took the surroundings into

Hoppy (Boyd) and "Boots" McCready (King) in *Texas Trail*, the only film in the series shot outside California.

account, beginning with light-hearted banter in the Bar 20's breezy, tree-dotted meadows (which, in actuality, lined the edge of Russ Spainhower's Anchor Ranch) and ending with lethal violence in the desolate rock formations of the Black Buttes.

Critics reviewing the Hoppys invariably noticed the rugged beauty of the Lone Pine locations captured so skillfully by Harlan's camera work. Their appreciation of those "scenic backdrops" and "picturesque desert locations" frequently softened reviews that, one senses, might not have been as favorable had the films been shot on overly familiar locations such as Iverson's Ranch near Chatsworth. *Hopalong Rides Again* elicited favorable notices from both the trade press and newspaper scribes. *Variety* in particular noted that the series had "hit its stride." Paramount's publicity machine and

marketing savvy helped make the third-season opener a huge success.

The Sherman unit barely had time to catch its collective breath before traveling to Arizona the following month to shoot the only Hopalong Cassidy film made outside California. On July 9, 1937, nearly 60 cast and crew members arrived in Flagstaff and headed to Foxboro Ranches, an elaborate spread perched on a rim 7,000 feet above Sedona's Schnebly Hill. At one time a summer camp for boys from wealthy families, the complex had already been used as a location several times by Hollywood studios. With its huge fences and corrals constructed from enormous pine logs, Foxboro is easily recognizable to today's aficionados of old Western movies.

After shooting six days at Foxboro—which stood in for both the villain's ranch and a U. S. Cavalry

Rustlers stampede the herd in "Ghost Creek Canyon," which was actually known as Blue Canyon.

fort—the *Texas Trail* company moved to Tuba City, on the Navajo reservation about 80 miles north of Flagstaff. From there the Sherman unit went some 30-odd miles east to the remote, hauntingly beautiful Blue Canyon, to which Flagstaff resident Lee Doyle, a liaison to motion-picture companies filming in northern Arizona, brought more than 800 wild horses and several dozen locals who worked as extras for the shooting of an elaborate sequence involving the roundup of mustangs.

Billy King wore the same outfit he'd used in *Hopalong Rides Again* but played a different character: a boy named "Boots" McCready, the son of Fort Boone's commanding officer. *Texas Trail* opens in 1898, with the Spanish-American War already underway. Hoppy, Lucky, and Windy are training a company of volunteers in hopes of joining Teddy Roosevelt's Rough Riders, but their plans change when Major McCready summons Cassidy to give him a very special assignment. The Cavalry desperately needs horses, and McCready wants Hoppy and his men to round up a massive herd said to be near Ghost Creek Canyon, an eerie place where other cowboys have died while attempting to herd mustangs.

A disappointed but patriotic Cassidy accepts the assignment, which he has been urged to keep secret. McCready's son Boots wrongly suspects that Hoppy has lost his nerve, especially after the Bar 20 puncher is taunted by local rancher Black Jack Carson

A striking portrait of William Boyd and George Hayes, taken in Blue Canyon during production of *Texas Trail*.

(Alexander Cross). Lucky, too, is worried about losing face; his sweetheart, schoolmarm Barbara Allen (Judith Allen) is a boarder at Carson's Triple X spread. She learns that Carson secretly heads the gang of rustlers preying on ranchers attempting wild-horse roundups in Ghost Creek Canyon.

Carson and the gang get the drop on Cassidy and his men, making them captives and stealing the horses earmarked for delivery to Fort Boone. But Boots, who has followed his idol Hoppy to apologize for doubting him, manages to get the drop on the rustler chief's lookout and helps the Bar 20 boys free themselves. Following a climactic stampede and gun battle, Carson and his horse thieves are apprehended by Cavalrymen. Hoppy delivers the mustangs and the film ends with him, Lucky and Windy in uniform, ready to join the Rough Riders at last.

Texas Trail is an atypical Hoppy Western in several ways—in addition to its one-time-only location, the film had a one-time-only director, David Selman, who did a terrific job—but ranks among the best nonetheless. It sports a simple, direct plot and several nice action set pieces, including a suspenseful climax in which Hoppy, on foot in a narrow pass, holds off the entire Carson gang with nothing more than his two six-

Cast and crew of *Heart of Arizona* posing at mine location near Lone Pine. Boyd in middle; note his stunt double fifth from left.

guns. Selman and cinematographer Russell Harlan milked the magnificent Arizona countryside for every drop of pictorial beauty. The shot compositions and camerawork left nothing to be desired, and on the big screen the results were literally breathtaking. Even today, viewed on TV screens from a videotape or DVD copy, *Texas Trail* impresses. At a taut 56 minutes the picture never flags for a minute. Best of all, it unfolds entirely in exterior settings.

Billy King remembered the Arizona location as "beautiful … just a fantastic place." Grace Bradley Boyd, who met her husband in Flagstaff and accompanied him to Tuba City for the remainder of the shoot, recalled in a 2005 interview with *Sedona Magazine* editor Joe McNeill that the summer heat—which topped 115 degrees—took a toll on cast and crew, especially George Hayes.

Hayes actually left the Hopalong Cassidy company for a while after the completion of *Texas Trail*: He was embroiled in a contract dispute with Pop Sherman. The next two installments in the series—1938's *Partners of the Plains* and *Cassidy of Bar 20*—featured Harvey Clark and Frank Darien as Hoppy's sidekicks. Neither was particularly effective,

and Sherman quickly resolved the dispute with Hayes, who returned for the fifth 1937-38 offering, *Heart of Arizona*. That film also marked Billy King's return to the series and his second appearance as Artie Peters.

Artie has returned to the West for another vacation with his uncle Buck (now played by John Elliott, since Duncan was temporarily unavailable). His arrival coincides with that of Belle Starr (Natalie Moorhead), recently released from prison after serving a five-year stretch for helping her rustler husband—since deceased—fend off lawmen. When the stagecoach taking her home stops to pick up Artie, it is met by Sheriff Hawley (John Beach), who believes she will take up criminal activities and wants her to keep going south, to a sleazy border town. Hopalong Cassidy loans Belle his horse so that she can complete the journey to her home in Gunsmoke Canyon, nestled in the majestic Sentinel Rocks country. What's left of her ranch is being run by now-fully-grown daughter Jackie (Dorothy Short) and her old foreman Ringo (Alden Chase).

Back at the Bar 20, Buck entrusts Lucky and a new man, Twister (Leo McMahon), with the job of

Hoppy refuses to believe the wounded Lucky guilty of rustling in *Heart of Arizona* (1938). John Beach as the sheriff.

bringing a herd of pure-bred cattle to market. The latter is secretly working with Ringo and his gang of rustlers, and his shifty demeanor has made Hoppy suspicious. But without proof of illegality he has no basis on which to denounce the puncher to Buck, who considers Twister a good cowhand.

While on the drive Lucky, who has developed a sudden infatuation with Jackie Starr, rides over to Gunsmoke Canyon to pay her a visit. Seeing an opportunity, Ringo and Twister rustle the herd and Lucky gets the blame. Sheriff Hawley arrests the love-struck puncher but Hoppy's young pal escapes, riding back to Belle and Jackie, and Buck refuses to press charges.

Twister is double-crossed and murdered by his partners, Ringo and cattle buyer "Trimmer" Winkler, on whose property stolen cattle have been butchered and their carcasses destroyed with quicklime. Hoppy and Windy uncover clues that lead them to Winkler's

mine, where they find the grisly remains of rustled stock. Meanwhile, Sheriff Hawley believes Lucky guilty of Twister's murder and goes to Belle's ranch to arrest him. In the ensuing fracas Lucky is wounded. Hoppy arrives in time to persuade the Sheriff that his young sidekick was in Gunsmoke Canyon the night Twister was murdered.

It becomes apparent that Ringo and Winkler are working together, and Hoppy proves it by marking a few head of Belle's unbranded cattle in such a way that they can be identified by someone who knows what to look for. Ringo eventually runs off her herd and delivers the stolen cows to Winkler, but his perfidy is discovered when Hoppy identifies the marked stock.

The rustlers corner Hoppy, Belle, and Jackie and pin them down with a barrage of gunfire. Windy, who has been wounded, makes his way to a predetermined spot high in the Sentinel Rocks and

Hoppy, Lucky, Windy, Buck (behind Hoppy, and played in this film by John Elliott), the other Bar 20 hands, and the sheriff seem to be reacting to something in *Heart of Arizona*, but this scene does not appear in the film.

signals the Bar 20, in the valley below, with a mirror that reflects the bright sunlight for miles. Artie, who has been manning a similar mirror at Buck's ranch night and day, receives the signal and summons his uncle, who mobilizes the Bar 20 punchers and rides to the rescue.

In order to have a showdown with the treacherous foreman in whom she had placed her trust for so many years, Belle emerges from cover and strides toward Ringo, who shoots her down. Hopalong settles the score but is wounded in the process. The remaining rustlers are about to close in when the Bar 20 men arrive. The mortally wounded Belle dies in Hoppy's arms, but not before begging him to bury her there, among the Sentinels she loves so much. The closing sequence shows Belle in her final resting place, framed by the magnificent mountains.

Heart of Arizona, made from an original screenplay by Norman Houston, is not only an excellent Hopalong Cassidy Western, it's a veritable love letter to Lone Pine's Alabama Hills. Houston's script was constructed without any scenes taking place in interiors, so the entire story unfolds outdoors. Dialogue scenes showing the wounded Lucky being nursed by Jackie could easily have been set inside Belle's ranch house (which is "played" by the Hoppy Cabin on Tuttle Creek Road), but instead they are staged on the porch, where Lucky rests in a chair to get sunlight and fresh air. During the course of the film Belle delivers an impassioned soliloquy expressing her love for the stately, imposing Sentinel Rocks that surround her modest spread. Few "B" Westerns have ever employed Lone Pine to greater advantage, or with more deliberation. In *Heart of Arizona* the Alabama Hills aren't just pretty props used to dress up the frame, they are an integral part of the story. You might even say they are the soul of the picture. Natalie Moorhead, who spent most of her career playing "the other woman" in society dramas, may have been an odd casting choice by Harry Sherman, but she did a marvelous job of conveying Belle Starr's enduring love for her majestic surroundings. For their part, director Les Selander and cinematographer Russell Harlan supplied more varied and striking views of the Alabams than had yet been seen in a Hopalong Cassidy film.

Billy King again played a small but pivotal role in the proceedings. Scattered lines of dialogue early on refer to him as a "pest" and a "nuisance," but as

Riding shotgun on the stage driven by Windy, Lucky has been wounded in a holdup in this scene from *Pride of the West* (1938). Charlotte Field and Billy King, playing brother and sister, can be seen at bottom right.

in *Hopalong Rides Again* it's made clear that the Bar 20 hands have an underlying respect and affection for him. And he justifies that respect by patiently standing guard over the signal mirror, even when it seems unlikely that Windy will be able to contact him. It's only when Artie receives the long-delayed signal that Buck and the boys are able to ride to the rescue.

King's last Hoppy was also the least impressive, although *Hopalong Rides Again*, *Texas Trail*, and *Heart of Arizona* had set the bar very high. It would have been tough for any production unit to consistently meet such lofty standards. As it happened, *Pride of the West* was made at a time when Paramount was pressuring Harry Sherman to trim the Hoppy budgets. Sherman's New York-based partner, J. D. "Jack" Trop, was sufficiently fearful of the outcome to head west and involve himself in production, at least temporarily. *Pride of the West* was conceived and developed with economy in mind. It lacked the scope and scale of previous series entries; even the story was routine and lacking in the little extra touches that, along with the strong production values, had made the Hopalong Cassidy Westerns tops in their field.

The yarn opens with Windy and Lucky employed by a stage line and driving into the town of Glenby after having been robbed of a gold shipment worth $20,000. Neither man is able to identify the robbers. Only bank president Caldwell (Kenneth Harlan) and sheriff Martin (Earle Hodgins) knew that the gold was being shipped, and the latter's failure to track down the bandits leads some to believe that he might be implicated. The robbery has dire consequences for local ranchers, because the gold was intended to back loans they had arranged with Caldwell. Real-estate agent Nixon, to whom most of the ranchers are in debt, now threatens to seize their property.

Martin's children Mary (Charlotte Field) and Dick (Billy King) ride out of town to find Hopalong Cassidy, engaged in a cattle roundup, and beg him for help. In typical "B"-Western fashion, the robbery is found to have derived from a plot concocted by Caldwell and Nixon to gain control of all local ranches and thus secure water rights in the entire district.

With Dick assisting him, Hoppy eventually locates the stolen gold and devises a plan to flush out and capture the thieves. The boy also helps him by watching a cabin where the bandits are hiding.

Pride of the West: Hoppy addresses Dick Martin in the sheriff's office as Windy and Lucky look on.

And he even frees Cassidy after the latter has been captured and tied up by Nixon and Caldwell. The banker, the real-estate agent, and their hired bandits are apprehended in a none-too-thrilling finale.

The film's working title was *Beneath Western Skies*; why it was changed to *Pride of the West* is anybody's guess. Nate Watt, who had directed the second sextet of Hoppys, wrote the screenplay. Reflecting the recent budgetary concerns, it eschewed the last-reel, mass-action climax that fans of the series had come to expect. Too many scenes were staged on mundane interior sets: the banker's office, the sheriff's jail, a Chinaman's lunchroom. It was all rather pedestrian. Russell Hayden's Lucky, described as having been wounded in the off-screen gold robbery at the story's beginning, spent the entire picture with his arm in a sling. It's possible that Hayden was injured early in production and portions of the script rewritten to compensate for his sidelining. Billy King and his horse Tony, however, were prominently featured. While not one of the very best films in the series,

Pride certainly gave the young rodeo star plenty of scenes in which to shine. And he did.

Perhaps the most notable thing about *Pride of the West* was its acknowledgment of the area in which it was produced This legend appeared in the opening credits: "Photographed near Lone Pine, California in the shadow of majestic Mt. Whitney." Hopalong Cassidy fans finally learned where so many their hero's adventures had been captured by movie cameras.

Completion of the picture marked an end to Billy King's contractual obligation to Pop Sherman. He retired from acting and eventually became an educator. But he continues to cherish his association with the most famous "B" Western series ever made. "I had a blast," he admitted recently to *Lone Pine in the Movies*. "The whole thing—being out in the rocks, being with all those great people. When I went into it I had no idea what an undertaking it is to make movies. But I loved it. And how many kids ever get to work alongside their idol?"   □□□

DON MURRAY:
FROM HELL TO TEXAS—
AND BACK TO LONE PINE

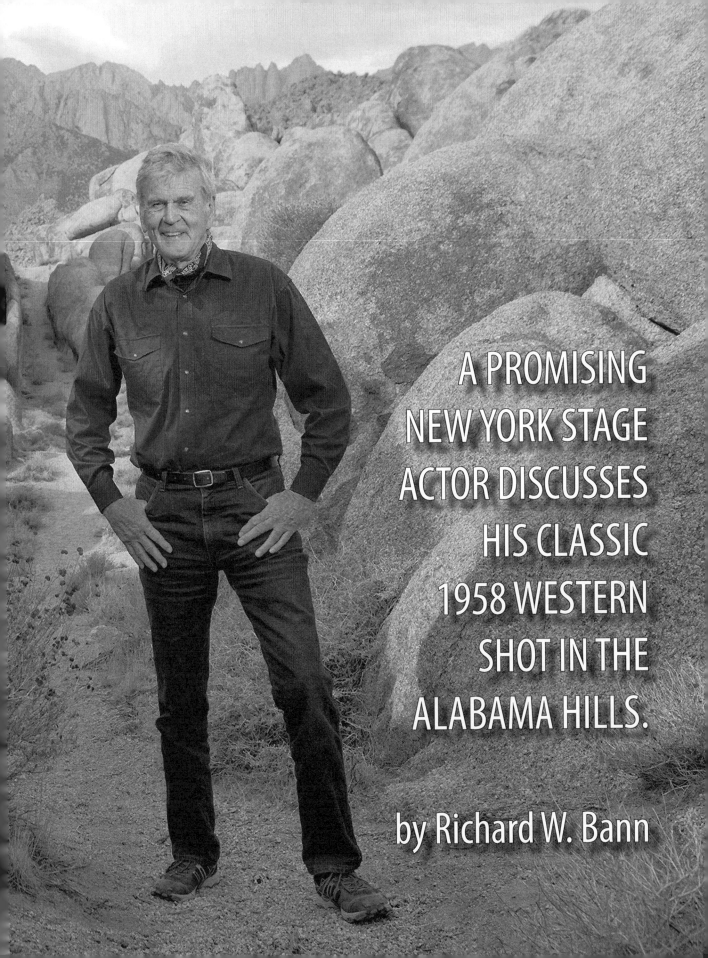

A PROMISING NEW YORK STAGE ACTOR DISCUSSES HIS CLASSIC 1958 WESTERN SHOT IN THE ALABAMA HILLS.

by Richard W. Bann

In 1956 the biggest star in Hollywood quit movies to study "serious" acting in New York. When she returned to 20th Century-Fox some 18 months later, Marilyn Monroe selected *Bus Stop*, based on the Broadway show, as her comeback showcase. Fox cast a stage actor of seven years' experience named Don Murray to play her leading man, and signed him to a six-year term contract. For his screen debut as a boyish, exuberant, rodeo cowboy, Murray earned an Oscar nomination. He thought Monroe was a terrific actress, but completely undisciplined, and terrified of acting. Murray was more interested personally in one the supporting actresses he met, Hope Lange. He later married her.

In a career that endures to this day, Don Murray would return to the stage and also perform on television, notably portraying Robert Kennedy in the 1974 TV movie *The Sex Symbol*. He would also write, produce, direct, or most often act in such notable theatrical films as *The Bachelor Party* (1957), *The Hoodlum Priest* (1961), and *Advise and Consent* (1962). He turned down the Paul Newman role opposite Elizabeth Taylor in *Cat on a Hot Tin Roof* (1958).

In the fall of 1957, for his fourth movie role, again cast as a cowboy, the then-28-year-old Murray visited Lone Pine to perform on location in the Alabama Hills of the Sierra Nevada Mountains.

Earlier, on March 4, 1957, 20th Century-Fox had announced to the Hollywood trade papers that the

Don Murray gives a good shaking to Marilyn Monroe in his breakout film, *Bus Stop* (1956).

studio had purchased a forthcoming Norton & Co. novel, Charles O. Locke's *The Hell-Bent Kid*, as a starring vehicle for Murray.

"I was very enthusiastic about [the project] because I liked the non-violent theme of the main character," Murray, a conscientious objector during the Korean War, recalled for Ed Hulse in an interview at the 2012 Lone Pine Film Festival. "All this killing was against the main character's will, and there wasn't anything he did for revenge or anything like that. I thought it was a very interesting expression of some sociological ideas, religious ideas. It was a concept that I believed in, and wanted to do."

The literary property, exploited as an "exciting character study," was to be adapted as a chase-and-vendetta Western film. Murray's naïve, pacifist-

A nice portrait of handsome Don Murray taken in Lone Pine during production of *From Hell to Texas* (1958).

leaning, bible-reading character is unjustly accused of knifing and killing the eldest son of a wealthy cattle rancher, forcing him to go on the run hoping to clear his name and save his life. The deceased's family seeks vengeance and mounts a massive manhunt, pursuing the guiltless Murray for retribution throughout the badlands of New Mexico, which happen also to be populated by hostile Comanche Indians. Locke's book—grimmer than the screenplay—takes a stand against violence, offering a protagonist with expertise as a rifleman who is nevertheless someone of high moral character, reluctant to use his weapon except in self-defense, as a last resort.

Long-time production chief Darryl F. Zanuck was then still presiding over Fox's fortunes and assigned Robert Buckner to produce *The Hell-Bent Kid*. Stating he hoped to make a tense Western reflecting "realism," Buckner set to work on a screen adaptation almost immediately in mid-March of 1957. First at Warner Bros., then at Fox, Buckner enjoyed a long career writing and producing for movies and television, with credits including screenplays for *Dodge City* (1939) and *Santa Fe Trail* (1940), as well as the original story for *Yankee Doodle Dandy* (1942), for which he earned an Academy Award nomination. Buckner served as producer on *Gentleman Jim* the same year.

By 1957, series "B" Westerns were finished in theaters but, happily, this remained a boom period for the genre as old film libraries were being syndicated in local television markets everywhere. Prime-time network TV schedules were filled with more serious, adult Westerns. Movie studios, too, were aiming at Westerns with more advanced moral complexity. Fox had slated several of these efforts for its upcoming season of releases.

On May 22, the working title on one of these projects, *The Hell-Bent Kid*, was changed to *Quick Draw at Fort Smith*. Four years earlier Columbia Pictures issued the smash hit *From Here to Eternity*, and during the summer someone at Fox liked the sound of that and came up with *From Hell to Texas* as the final working title. Unfortunately, this gave some movie patrons and critics the impression of a lesser kind of picture, rather than the thoughtful and outstanding film it turned out to be.

Assigned to wield the megaphone was the capable and versatile veteran of big action-adventure films,

Henry Hathaway. Once a kid actor in silent films, Hathaway advanced through the ranks into a 40-year career as a tough, workhorse director. He made prestige films with Marilyn Monroe, Mae West, Shirley Temple, Carole Lombard, Gary Cooper, Henry Fonda, Tyrone Power, and several with John Wayne.

The unpretentious Hathaway had been to Lone Pine before, having lensed such outdoor sagas as *The Thundering Herd* (1933), *Lives of a Bengal Lancer* (1935, and for which he was Oscar-nominated), *Brigham Young* (1940), and *Rawhide* (1951), all at least partially filmed in the shadow of Mount Whitney. Later this 59-year-old stern taskmaster would return to the region for *North to Alaska* (1960), *How the West Was Won* (1963) and *Nevada Smith* (1966).

"To be a good director you've got to be a bastard," the fiery Hathaway once said, acknowledging his colorful temper tantrums. "I'm a bastard and I know it." Plenty of Hollywood insiders knew it too, and warned Don Murray what he was in for. "Other actors were telling me, 'Oh, my God, he's a horror,'" Murray remembered. " 'He yells and screams. He's really some difficult kind of man.'

"So I had my first meeting with him, and I walked into his office at Fox. He's sitting in his chair, and he's smoking this cigar. And he just looks at me. So I sit down, next to him, in the chair. He doesn't say anything. He doesn't introduce himself, or say 'Hello, Don,' or anything. He just stares at me, puffing on his cigar. So I sat there, and I stared at him! I never said hello to *him*. So he stared. And I stared. Just like a couple of kids, you know? Finally he takes his cigar out of his mouth, and says, 'Well, what do you think of the script?' I said, 'I don't think it's nearly as good as the book, but I think you're going to make a good movie out of it.' So he says, 'So do I,' and 'Let's go to work.' I never had any problem with him at all!"

During the pre-production period, Murray was asked his opinion of Buckner's story treatment. "I didn't think it caught the depth of the character the way the book did," Murray explained. "I told that to Henry Hathaway, and he agreed with me. So they hired Wendell Mayes, and Wendell Mayes really caught it. I didn't have to bring anything more to this movie than he already put into the script. I just fulfilled what he wrote."

Mayes' screenplay credits include *The Spirit of St. Louis* (1957), *Anatomy of a Murder* (1959), *Advise and Consent* (1962), *The Poseidon Adventure* (1972, which earned him an Oscar nomination), and *Death Wish* (1974).

For a 1971 piece in *Focus on Film*, Mayes told Rui Nogueira that Hathaway was "very easy for a writer to work with. He's absolutely dreadful for actors to work with. He's probably the toughest son of a bitch in Hollywood. He is tough for a reason. Hathaway is not the most articulate man in the world and he maintains control of his set and of his crew and his actors by being cantankerous and rather cruel sometimes. He knows what he's doing; he isn't doing it out of hand. He's doing it deliberately because this is the way he's discovered he can work. It isn't true with the writer. He's a very gentle man when you sit down with him in a room to write. He doesn't feel he has to browbeat you."

Story development and casting continued into the summer months of 1957. Tall, 20-year-old Diane Varsi, another newcomer, was hired to play the hoydenish adopted daughter. This introverted product of a broken home was then already twice married with a child. Raised by strangers and sent to convents, Varsi wed first at 15. In high school, she failed all her studies, dropped out in her junior year, and hitchhiked to Hollywood from San Mateo, California.

Diane Varsi began her entertainment career as a folk singer who played bongo drums, but then she began to study acting with Jeff Corey. He recommended her for a prime role as Lana Turner's troubled daughter in *Peyton Place* (1957). That Varsi and her character were both a little mixed up may have helped the actress earn an Academy Award nomination in her first screen appearance. Next, she signed a term contract with Fox and played Gary

Tod Lohman (Murray) says goodbye to Amos Bradley (Chill Wills) and daughter Juanita (Diane Varsi) in *From Hell to Texas*.

Cooper's daughter in *Ten North Frederick* (1958). Despite bouts of temperament, repeated disavowals of stardom, and having stated that she found acting "personally destructive," Varsi was nevertheless hailed by gossip columnist Hedda Hopper as "the most interesting [film] personality of 1958." Reporter Joe Hyams thought she was "the Marlon Brando of actresses."

Texas-born character actor Chill Wills, then age 54, was signed by producer Buckner for a key role as the kindly rancher and Varsi's father, to be billed third. Wills was prone to outrageous scene stealing, but Hathaway kept him in check.

Chill had been in show business all his life, starting out as a child actor in tent shows. During the Depression, Wills formed a singing group for which he performed as bass vocalist: Chill Wills and the Avalon Boys. They worked in movies with Laurel & Hardy, also with William Boyd early on in his Hopalong Cassidy series. The quartet disbanded

Despite his New York stage background, Murray made a surprisingly capable Western leading man.

in 1938 when Wills obtained regular work as George O'Brien's sidekick in the popular series this great Western performer was making for RKO. O'Brien liked to furnish his own comedy. After Wills chewed up the scenery in fine fashion for one of their pictures, the star came over to him and put his arm around Wills, who in 1976 quoted O'Brien as telling him, "Chill, you're going to do good in Western pictures, but you ain't going to be in no more of mine." O'Brien used to tell pretty much the same story.

Not a problem, as Wills went on to a long career supporting big names in important films, including several with John Wayne, one of which he was Oscar-nominated for, *The Alamo* (1960). And Wills' unique, gravelly speaking voice and delivery was secured to provide off-screen lines for Francis, the Talking Mule, in a popular series of Universal-International films.

"Chill Wills was such a wonderful man," as Don Murray recalled him. "I remember, I wasn't drinking any alcohol at that time. But he'd say, in the evening, after shooting, 'Come on over into my room, I got some Jack Daniels here.' I said, 'What's Jack Daniels?' He said, 'Oh, it's God's nectar, son, it's God's nectar. It's Tennessee sippin' whiskey.' And he'd describe Jack Daniels, and sipping it, and how it feels in your throat. He really wanted to make me a drinker!"

(There is a scene in *From Hell to Texas* during which the warm and easy Wills offers an unspecified brand of whiskey to Murray, who drinks it reluctantly, saying, "I ain't much for whiskey.")

"He had such an unctuous way of talking," Murray said of Wills. "He did an interview with Joe Hyams, one of the major syndicated writers about movies. Hyams asked him how he lasted so long in the industry. Wills told him, 'By not being a leading man,' he said. 'I don't have the success or failure of the film on my soul. I just walk in, say my lines, stand in the right place. I ride the horse the right way. I leave it to the young fellahs like that—you see that fellah standing over there? Well, that Don Murray, he can out-drill ya, he can out-draw ya, and he can out-ride ya. You gotta just *smooth* back, and let him go.' Well, truth was, I couldn't do any of those things. I couldn't out-anything Chill Wills! He was one of the greatest. *That's* why he lasted so long in the industry."

Signed to play Wills' wife in *From Hell to Texas* was the Mexican dancer-actress, Margo, at the time

Beset with personal problems during shooting, Diane Varsi nonetheless gave a memorable performance.

Mrs. Eddie Albert. For show-business billing she had dramatically shortened her given name, which was Marie Marguerita Guadalupe Teresa Estela Bolado Castilla y O'Donnell. Rita Hayworth's father taught her to dance as a child. Margo's uncle was bandleader Xavier Cugat, and she performed with his group for years. In films since 1934, she made her most memorable impression in a scene from *Lost Horizon* (1937), in which her character departed Shangri-La's protected environment to suddenly age and die, a startling transformation from young beauty to withered old woman.

For the fourth-billed role, Warner Bros. was persuaded to loan Fox a rebellious, 21-year-old actor with a violent temper named Dennis Hopper. Troubled by drugs and alcohol abuse at the outset of a wild, roller-coaster career, Hopper fancied himself as some kind of heir apparent to James Dean, with whom he had appeared in both *Rebel Without a Cause* (1955) and *Giant* (1956).

Juanita Bradley doesn't trust Tod Lohman even though her father clearly does.

"I imitated his style in art and in life," Hopper said of Dean. "It got me in a lot of trouble. Of his first film for Henry Hathaway the actor later recalled, "The part in *From Hell to Texas* was a weak son of the bad man, and I didn't want to do it, but the studio said go on and do it."

Hopper, like Dean, Marlon Brando, and Montgomery Clift, was a "method" actor, employing a technique derived from the teaching of a Russian director named Konstantin Stanislavsky. It was popularized by Lee Strasberg's Actors Studio in New York after World War II. Actors were encouraged to draw from their own experiences and use their private feelings to internalize a part and try to become the character. Old-school, old-hand, no-nonsense Hollywood types like Hathaway believed this realistic style of performing was dull, mannered, and a lot of nonsense. So there was bound to be conflict between the brutally frank,

dictatorial Hathaway and the anti-authoritarian Hopper.

Also in the cast: more familiar characters actors including the salty, craggy-featured Jay C. Flippen as a friendly itinerant trader; one of Sam Peckinpah's as well as Warren Beatty's favorites, the ever-menacing R. G. Armstrong, who as the vengeful, relentless cattle baron father has "a queer sense of justice;" and from John Ford's "company of heroes," likable Harry Carey, Jr., who had little to do here. Thus the picture offered a nice blend of seasoned veterans and fresh faces, which 20th Century-Fox would promote heavily, hoping they would click with the movie-going public. Murray and Varsi were accorded star billing, while Wills and Hopper were credited as co-stars.

Curiously, for all the attention given to Hopper, it is R. G. Armstrong as the vindictive, patriarchal oppressor who had the stronger role and turned in

The West's most savage man-chase..

FROM HELL TO TEXAS

STARRING
DON MURRAY · DIANE VARSI
CO-STARRING
CHILL WILLS · DENNIS HOPPER

20th Century-Fox
CINEMASCOPE
COLOR by DE LUXE

PRODUCED BY ROBERT BUCKNER · DIRECTED BY HENRY HATHAWAY · ROBERT BRUCKNER and WENDELL MAYES

the more memorable performance. Hopper seems to be pouting through scenes with his usual angst, but to little avail. Plus his small stature beneath a much-too-large Stetson works against him as a threat to Murray, or anyone else—particularly not to Hathaway as director.

Armstrong was new to pictures. He had earned a Masters degree in English, studied with Strasberg at the Actors Studio, and appeared on Broadway. Armstrong recalled, "During *From Hell to Texas*, Hathaway took me aside and said, 'You've got it in you

to be a good actor, but not if you don't stop leaving your lines up on the end when you're talking.' Well, that was something I could work on, and I did."

Armstrong died at age 95, shortly before the 2012 Lone Pine Film Festival and just 24 days after the passing of his closest friend and college classmate, Andy Griffith.

Finally, on an approved budget of $1,382,000, the Hathaway company commenced principal photography on October 4, 1957. "It was not a low-budget film at all," Don Murray has affirmed. "It

00002-1

was a large-budget film. We really had time to do everything; there was nothing rushed."

The Hathaway company shot for 47 days and concluded production on December 4. Most of the exteriors were filmed, according to an interesting account in the studio pressbook, among "the rugged Sierra Nevadas near Lone Pine and Bishop, California, the picturesque Dry Lakes region north of Death Valley, the weird Sand Dunes country to the east, and in the Alabama Hills, at the foot of Mount Whitney.

"Working at elevations up to 8,000 feet, the company was snowed out for a time," the account furnished by the Fox studio publicity department continued. "Even as locations go in such rough terrain, it was a tough one. When the snow let up, the icy wind howled for days, to the point where it was difficult to record dialogue for even the close-ups. At one time or another during the five weather-battered weeks of location, nearly every member of the cast and crew was down with flu except Don Murray and 57-year-old director Hathaway.

"Diane Varsi suffered bad windburns. So, to everyone's surprise including his, did leatherish Chill Wills, who worked *sans* makeup, which would have afforded a degree of protection against the blasts.

"The $500 worth of cowpoke duds bought by 20th for Don Murray to wear in his role were promptly aged to look like something hanging in a secondhand clothing store. Chaps were scuffed with abrasives, shirts aged with chemicals in the wardrobe man's 'time-bucket,' hat stained and dust-blasted to a convincing state of disreputability.

"For veteran director Henry Hathaway the location at Lone Pine was like coming home. He's not sure just how many movies he's made in that country, including *Lives of a Bengal Lancer*, a movie milestone of 1935. Said Hathaway, gazing at the weirdly worn formations of the Alabama Hills near Lone Pine: 'These rocks have been worn down to their roots by time, erosion, and the hooves of Hollywood horses.'

"However, Hathaway also found in the region any number of colorful areas never before caught by the cameras, such as the Hot Sulphur Springs, where at 7,000 feet, the water comes boiling out of the rocks. It was near here the scenes were filmed in which Diane Varsi shocks Murray by taking a bath in the stream, later keeps him partially submerged as she launders his clothes.

"For the scene in which Dennis Hopper's clothes catch fire during a gunfight, a suit of asbestos underwear was made for the actor, and his face was covered with transparent unguents. Despite the realism of the sequence, only damage sustained by Hopper in the scene was a pair of badly singed eyelashes."

Varsi's nude swimming scene echoes one of Hathaway's early pre-Code Zane Grey Westerns, the exceptional *To the Last Man* (1933), which finds Esther Ralston similarly unashamed to bathe in the nude despite the presence of a male onlooker. And *From Hell to Texas* carries a theme found in several Hathaway films: heroes compelled by circumstances to resort to violence as a means of resolving conflict. His earlier efforts *13 Rue Madeleine* (1946), *Rawhide* (1951), and *Garden of Evil* (1954) exploited this concept, as did *True Grit* (1969). The plot device was introduced to Hathaway—and impressed him—when he worked as assistant director on the 1929 version of *The Virginian* starring Gary Cooper. Hathaway acknowledged this fact regularly in interviews over the years.

Murray's recollection of shooting conditions was that they were less severe than as stated in studio publicity: "We really didn't have weather problems," he declared last year when visiting Lone Pine. "We were up here in the fall and the weather really didn't give us any problems at all. It was kind of cold, which made it pleasant for all the riding and so on. It was just really a perfect location." Murray added the temperature of the Hot Springs water he and Diane Varsi bathed in was nice and warm, even hot.

During the Lone Pine Film Festival of 2012, Don Murray revisited all of the film's key locations out in the Alabama Hills and environs. He told *Los Angeles Times* staff photographer Don Kelsen, "This place was a dream location for me when I was a kid, growing up watching favorites like Ken Maynard here, then going outside to act out our own scenes playing cowboys and Indians. So coming here fulfilled a boyhood dream."

Upon arrival in Lone Pine the production unit went right to work, from sun-up through sundown.

Don Murray as he looked in the late '70s and early '80s, around the time he appeared in *Knots Landing*.

Murray regales the audience with an anecdote during his interview at the 2012 Lone Pine Film Festival.

By summer's end, Buckner, Mayes and Hathaway had finished polishing the script and the company set out to shoot it, scene by scene, word for word. Nothing more, nothing less.

"Hathaway really knew what he was doing, and the writers knew what *they* were doing," Murray explained. "There was nothing experimental about this. As a matter of fact, the amazing thing [was that] this was the first film that I did where there wasn't a pre-production rehearsal period. When I stepped on the set of *From Hell to Texas*, the first scene that I did was the scene with Dennis Hopper where he tries to ambush me. It ends up with shooting the horse, and I end up wounding Dennis.

"Hathaway says, 'Okay, let's rehearse in front of the camera. You walk here, you walk here…'. And I said my lines, Dennis said his lines, and Hathaway says, 'Okay, let's roll 'em!' I said, 'What do you mean, let's roll 'em? Let's have a rehearsal!' Hathaway said, 'We just *had* a rehearsal.'

"So he was not a stage director, he was a movie director. That was something I had to adjust to immediately.

"But I tell you an interesting thing about that scene where I leap in the air and I shoot Dennis while I'm stretched out in the air in a sort of diving rifle shot. The first time I did it, Hathaway said, 'Cut, cut, cut. Don, point the gun at him. You're pointing off in the woods somewhere. Don't worry; it's a blank. You can't hurt him.' I said, 'I *was* pointing it at him.' He said, 'No, you weren't. You're pointing off in the woods.'

"So we do it again. I point the gun … bang! Hathaway says, 'Don, I told you, point the gun at him. You can't hurt him. It's a blank, you're pointing it away from him.' I said again, 'No, I was pointing right at him.' He said, 'No, you weren't. Do it again!'

"So okay, we did it a third time. And the same thing. He said, 'Don….' And as he's balling me out this time, and I'm insisting I pointed the gun right

While in Lone Pine for the Film Festival, Don revisited locations where *From Hell to Texas* was shot.

at the guy, Dennis Hopper comes walking in, and he comes up to Hathaway, and he says, 'Henry…' and he is bleeding right down from over his left eye and onto his cheek. And he's got, like, a little hole, and he is pointing over his left eye, where the cardboard wad from the blank hit him right above that eye. It could have put his eye out, if it had been a little lower. Henry Hathaway just walked away, totally embarrassed."

Murray's line to Hopper in the scene: "I could've put a bullet right between your eyes." By then Murray was a deadeye shot and he nearly did. Only a few weeks further into the production, Hopper would be set on fire and have his eyelashes singed, to add to being shot over the eye, drawing blood streaming down his face. The journey from Hell to Texas, however, was just beginning for Hopper.

Day by day, the filmmaking experience of being outside, on location in Lone Pine, helped to inform Murray's performance and shape his character. It was quite a change for an actor used to working on stage and television in cramped sets. "It helps enormously to have the real sets, the real circumstances around," Murray explained. "Being out in the Alabama Hills just gave you such a wonderful feeling of this cowboy, because my life had been completely the opposite of that.

"I think that was one of the most important things for me, to get the feeling of being a cowboy, of being out in the Alabama Hills, around those rocks. And also being with Western people, getting the feeling, almost, that I was brought up by these people, in these hills. *From Hell to Texas* would not have been the kind of film it was without being in Lone Pine.

Kent Sperring, Lone Pine festival attendee and location aficionado, often seen exploring the Alabama Hills for hidden movie sights is more than happy to share some of his most recent discoveries with festival guest star, Don Murray.

"When I played that cowboy in *Bus Stop*, I couldn't have been more ill-prepared for the role. I was a New Yorker, and had never been on a horse before. I had a New York accent. And I didn't have any preparation time for *Bus Stop*. I was hired, and within a week I was on the set doing the movie.

"I like to have time to study a role, to get into a role. I would like to have learned to ride a horse, or know something about rodeos. I knew nothing about that. But I had a wonderful writer in George Axelrod, and I had a fabulous director in Joshua Logan. I was nominated for an Academy Award, and if I'd won the Oscar I would have had to cut it in half to share with Josh Logan because that was more his performance than mine. I just followed his direction and did what he said.

"But in *From Hell to Texas*, I had a lot of preparation. They crafted the film for me. And I had to craft myself to fit the form, the role. The first thing I did, I worked with a wonderful teacher named Bob Adler, who taught me to ride. As he said, 'I'm gonna teach you to ride a horse, not a saddle.' He started me bareback. He made me learn how to take care of the horse, to clean his hooves, and to clean his bridle, and not only to wash him down, but to do anything and everything that a cowboy does to take care of his horse. We had a couple months working on doing that.

"And then maybe the most important thing was that a great cowboy named Rodd Redwing—who was actually a full-blooded Indian—taught me the rifle work. He taught me to use the rifle like a pistol. So many things that the cowboy does with that rifle are so fast that you don't really see what he's doing. Like in the bar when he's facing the Mexican with the big hat called Bayliss (Rodolfo Acosta), I'm actually holding the rifle upside down by the loop, and when I pick it up, it looks like I just pick it up and point to him. But actually what I'm doing is I'm throwing it out and loading it, and pulling it back, and dropping it, and catching it. But it all happens so fast, due to his teaching, that you don't really see what is happening. That is a very important part of the film, that this guy is so lethal, because he handles that gun like he was born with it. It's almost like another hand that he had. So that was the kind of preparation we had for the film. But other people did that for me. I couldn't have done that myself."

When the technical advisor, Rodd Redwing, learned how Murray's non-violence beliefs paralleled those of his easygoing film character, the Chickasaw Indian shook his head, sadly, and said, "What a waste! The boy is a natural. He has learned to handle a rifle better than any man I've ever instructed."

Back at the Fox studio one day, former musical-comedy actor turned private-eye tough guy Dick Powell happened to see Redwing rehearsing with Murray as he perfected his marksmanship and lightning-quick handling of a Winchester rifle. Powell was so impressed at what he saw—all the tricks and fast action—it gave him the idea. He was then a top producer running Four Star Television, and watching Murray gave him an idea for a new TV series. When Murray expressed disinterest in doing television, Powell hired Chuck Connors instead, to star as *The Rifleman*. The show was soon a big hit and ran for five years. Coincidentally *The Rifleman* often featured villainy furnished by Murray's *Texas* castmate R. G. Armstrong. Co-star Johnny Crawford, who played Connor's son in the series, never knew this story until he heard it at last year's Lone Pine Film Festival.

Other instructors and stunt men serving Murray and the rest of the company behind the scenes included several names known and respected by serious fans of action movies going way back in film history: Cliff Lyons and David Sharpe, also past Lone Pine Film Festival guests Loren Janes and Tap (son of Yakima) Canutt. The latter performed one of his father's signature daring feats with a stagecoach and its team of racing horses. Plus the picture's second unit director was Richard Talmadge, who had doubled for no less than Douglas Fairbanks in classic silent films four decades earlier, and also starred in action-adventure films of his own. So Don Murray may have been new to this field, but he was surrounded by the absolute best, most seasoned veterans of outdoor Western and serial movies— motion pictures that *moved*.

Locally, support came from the one liaison that motion-picture people always relied upon for horses, cattle, rolling stock, locations, etc., in Lone Pine: Russ Spainhower, owner of the Anchor Ranch. As things turned out, *From Hell to Texas* was the last production Spainhower served on. "Henry Hathaway really wanted him on that," daughter Joy Anderson told Lone Pine historian Dave Holland. "That was 1957, the year he died." Spainhower's Anchor Ranch was used for scenes depicting home life for Chill Wills' character and his large family.

The film production's most dramatic conflict was not part of the plot. It was never photographed. It was the clash of generations and styles and egos and pathologies, between two stubborn men with ferocious reputations for their emotional outbreaks and yelling: Dennis Hopper, a young, "method actor" with an entitlement complex, versus Henry Hathaway, an old school, volatile director with a dictator complex who was used to getting his way.

"It was a major fight," Hopper told author Peter L. Winkler. "We fought and fought throughout the whole picture. He wanted me. He thought I was the best young actor he'd seen. But he wanted me to imitate Marlon Brando in timing and gestures, and he gave me line readings and his approach to acting. I walked off the picture three times."

Don Murray remembers, "There was a lot of trouble between Henry Hathaway and Dennis Hopper. Dennis has written about it and talked about it in many interviews. He was then deeply into drugs and all sorts of self-destructive things. He was a very, very difficult person. And Henry, I think, behaved very admirably with him, treated Dennis with great patience. You can see that he got a very good performance out of him. But it was hard for Henry to get that performance, because of Dennis's attitude.

"As a matter of fact, one day Hathaway came and knocked on my door and said, 'Don, I just don't know what to do, I've never seen … I've never had an actor react like this. He's swearing at me, he's refusing to do what I ask him to do. I am at my wits end. I don't know what to do.'

"What I would say to Hathaway is to exercise patience and just keep on going for what he wants. The very rebellious nature that Dennis Hopper has as a person is exactly what the role has. He's the spoiled brat of a wealthy rancher who's justifiably started a vendetta against my character and is very, very undisciplined and a brat, but that's the quality you want to get from him, you want to use that quality. I think that Hopper ended up very good in

the film because that's exactly what comes across in the film."

The first time Hopper stormed off the picture, Murray recommended Hathaway meet with the mercurial actor away from the set to address their problems. They went to dinner in restaurants in both Hollywood and Lone Pine. Evidently each time Hathaway was uncharacteristically charming and understanding when Hopper would plead his case for method acting and how he foresaw doing the next day's scenes. By Hopper's account, Hathaway was nearly begging the actor to come back. Yet when Hopper returned to work in the morning, the director reverted to behaving like a monster, yelling, screaming, and barking out different instructions in contravention of whatever had been agreed upon the night before. To get even, Hopper would ruin scenes on purpose, pulling stunts like leaving a paper cup within camera range.

"Once on a weekend I had a talk with Dennis," Murray remembered. "I tried to get to what was motivating him, why he was being so self-destructive. And so potentially destructive to the movie. I reminded him of the fine work he had done in *Rebel Without a Cause*, and how good he was in *Giant*. And how this film had the makings of being as good as those films, and he shouldn't do anything to disturb that—to hurt not only his own career but the film, too.

"I said, 'What is going on with you? What is in your head?' At last he broke down and told me he was going through a very emotional thing that day. He was having an affair with a married actress, and as a matter of fact, a couple of nights before I talked to him, the husband broke into his room and attacked him, and in defending himself, he was kicking at the fellow. The guy knocked him back on the bed, and picked up a chair, and was swinging at him, and almost broke his legs. He showed me that his legs were full of cuts and bruises and so on. He was almost crying. He was pouring himself out.

"Then I told him, 'People come with lots of problems into their daily lives and they have to live up to their responsibilities. One of the things that I held up to him was the stuntmen. I said these stuntmen do such a terrific job for us. They risk their lives, actually, to make a good movie, and I think you have got to lay down and lay aside your personal

L to R: Murray, Varsi, Wills.

Murray (left), Dennis Hopper.

problems, whatever they are, and come out and use the great talent that's been given to you.'

"I don't know if what I said had any great effect. But I think the act of pouring out his soul to me gave Dennis a kind of release and he started to behave much better on the film. The entire experience was torture for him."

When Murray told this story to a packed house after a screening of the picture at the 2012 Lone Pine Film Festival, interviewer Ed Hulse quipped, "I had no idea Dennis Hopper was going through such a tumultuous time; I mean, based on what you describe, being set on fire was probably a relief for him."

The last day on location, December 10, 1957, called for a ten-line scene with Hopper and Armstrong, who played his father in the picture. Hathaway began by pointing to stacks of film cans, indicating he had enough raw stock to shoot for another four months. He told Hopper the actor would finally do everything specifically and exactly as directed this time, or "you can make a career out of this one scene in this one movie because I own 40% of this studio."

In other words, *my way, or the 395 Highway*. It was 7 am. They were there for the duration. They worked all morning on the scene. Time after time, Hopper would fail to take direction from Hathaway. They sent out for lunch. They sent out for dinner. Soon executives were gathering to watch the grudge match

from the wings. This was big news, spreading fast. Calls were coming in from Warner Bros. Finally Jack Warner himself phoned and said to Hopper, "What the fuck is going on? Do what fucking Hathaway says, and get back over here."

It was 10 pm when Hopper conceded defeat. He was crying, a broken man. James Dean was dead, and Dennis Hopper wished *he* was too. It was at this point Hathaway made the statement that still echoes in infamy, to the point of becoming a Hollywood cliché. As the long day, and longer production on the picture wrapped, Hathaway walked slowly toward Hopper, and with his cigar bobbing between his lips announced for all to hear, "Kid, there's one thing I can promise you: You'll never work in this town again."

Fox immediately began post-production work on *From Hell to Texas*, and Warner Bros. promptly dropped Dennis Hopper from its list of contract players.

The picture had taken 47 days to shoot. The negative cost came in at $1,522,000. So they were $175,000, or almost 13 percent, over budget. How much was due to the various *contretemps* involving Hathaway and Hopper is anyone's guess.

While Hathaway had to be away from the studio for a while, he gave an assistant editor named Johnny Ehrin a chance to cut the picture together. Ehrin had been highly recommended. Hathaway told film historian Rudy Behlmer, "When I got back, I looked

Murray, Wills, Varsi.

Hopper, Ken Scott, Salvador Baguez.

at the picture, and oh boy, what a mess. I came out and I'm in a stupor. Somehow he missed the point. He let things run too long, he let things run too short. Anytime anything could be a judgment call, he was wrong. Then I got a call from Zanuck. He said, 'I understand the picture is cut. I'd like to see it Monday night.' I said, 'There's no way. I just saw the picture and it's a mess.' He said, 'You don't think I can fix what's wrong with it?' I said, 'No.' So he got sort of pissed off at me because he's the great cutter of all time. I saw it Thursday night and this is Friday morning. He said, 'I want to see it Monday night. I know about pictures. I saw the rushes, I saw the stuff.' "

Hathaway raced to find his regular editor, Barbara McLean, and together they sat at a Movieola from Friday afternoon through late Sunday running, re-running, and fixing the rough cut until it looked like another movie entirely. "Just a complete other picture," Hathaway recalled.

Fox created a publicity campaign to promote its two "new faces" belonging to Murray and Varsi. Would the public go for them? *Bus Stop* had given the young New York actor some cachet, but Marilyn Monroe had attracted the lion's share of attention. It remained to be seen whether he would be a box-office draw in his own right.

Promotion and publicity was plentiful. A special Popular Library edition of Locke's novel, now called a "Great Western Saga," was issued by Pines Publications to coincide with the release of the

picture and support all playdates. Press releases and advertising material were typically hyperbolic. Taglines written for them included these:

"You can't hunt a man like an animal without turning him into a beast."

"In the tradition of *Stagecoach, High Noon,* and *Shane* ... "

"No Mightier Adventure Ever Swept Out Of The Mighty West."

"Every Gun In The Territory Was Hired To Kill Him."

"The West's Most Savage Man-Chase... From Hell to Texas."

Most new movies were then being promoted with an industry-wide slogan to help reverse declining theater attendance and compete with the increasingly popular phenomenon of television: "Get more out of life.... Go out to a movie!" Republic Pictures had just left the movie business and was switching to TV production, while other studios experienced diminished box-office receipts as more and more people stayed home to watch television.

The film was previewed for the trade press in New York on April 11, 1958. The domestic release date was June 1. In England the picture was issued to theaters by 20th Century-Fox as *Manhunt* instead of *From Hell to Texas*.

As usual, *Variety*'s take on the picture was dead on: "Slick Western for action and drive-in markets; lacks marquee lure for deluxe spots ... crisp Western ... handsomely mounted in CinemaScope and De Luxe color. Reminiscent of Stanley Kramer's *High Noon* ... same kind of adult fare with a similar tension that builds throughout. Director Hathaway wrings suspense galore from the yarn as sharpshooting Murray manages to keep a whisker ahead of his pursuers.... What could be called 'High Moon' is a sock moonlit climax when Murray breaks up a tense gun duel by suddenly dropping his rifle to save Armstrong's sole remaining son, Dennis Hopper, from a flaming death. Murray turns in a taut and gripping performance. Less impressive, however, is Miss Varsi, who's pretty but not quite the frontier type. Hopper occasionally over-acts. Outdoor vistas, lushly photographed, are frequently eye filling on the Cinemascope screen."

From the notice filed for *The Hollywood Reporter*: "Thrilling stunt work that includes a man being trampled by a stampede of horses and another emerging from a gunfight with flaming clothes makes *From Hell to Texas* a more than satisfactory offering for action fans. Production also has the advantage of beautifully rugged locations. This gives it a spacious and bracing outdoor flavor.... Things are kept from being too melodramatic by Murray's underplaying until he seems like the cowboy next door.... Diane Varsi produces some very amusing snippy humor as (Chill Wills's) bossy daughter."

Film Daily hailed *From Hell to Texas* as "An unusually good Western, ranks among the best of the year in its category. It has a splendid cast headed by Don Murray and Diane Varsi, and its story is one of robust action and gunplay that always has a feeling of realism at its core.... It has a blazing climax and the ending is a surprise one."

Motion Picture Herald complimented the "taut and compelling screenplay, as played out against the utterly breathtaking backgrounds of some of the west's most magnificent scenery. Here is exciting action material, tightly knit and beautifully set, which should attract wide appreciative audiences."

In Los Angeles, those audiences flocked to 18 theaters when the picture opened there in early June.

"Despite that spine-grating, hackneyed title," said the *Los Angeles Times* in its review, "*From Hell to Texas* is one of the most intelligent Westerns turned out in a long time.... Performances are excellent; Murray is a very warm, very gentle type of cowboy; Miss Varsi is, of course, a very sensitive performer."

The paper praised the "intelligent, cliché-free script," but reflected the sentiments of several critics who thought Varsi was "mannish," Murray "virginally modest," and the leads as a romantic couple "bland," their love scenes "cloying." That the public thought so too may well explain the disappointing worldwide revenue, reported as $2,643,000 (at a time when the average admission ticket price was 51 cents) and producing a net loss of $346,000. Even if Hathaway's production unit had averted a budget overrun, the picture would have failed to recoup its cost, being overlooked in a year with so many other Westerns, headed up by William Wyler's *The Big Country*. The top two stars who *did* attract big numbers at the box office that year were Glenn Ford and Elizabeth Taylor.

Today the consensus seems to be that this hard-to-find film remains underrated, and will surprise audiences. "An unsung beauty," was the term applied by film historian William K. Everson, who went on to say: "The script for *From Hell to Texas* was an unusually literate one, coming up with the expected action yet at the same time avoiding hackneyed characters and situations. Even the badmen, as vicious a family as we had seen on the screen since John Ford had delighted us with the Clantons and the Cleggs, act with a certain logic and justification, and aren't even villains in the strictest sense of the word. Don Murray was particularly well cast in the lead, the kind of role that Audie Murphy was always looking for at Universal and never quite finding.

"Hathaway seemed to have combined, successfully, much of the old William S. Hart sentiment and austerity with the slickness of John Ford, which is perhaps why in 'look' and appeal [*From Hell to Texas*] so much resembles Ford's late Western silent, *Three Bad Men*. The film has some magnificent outdoor locations—ramshackle towns and single frame buildings rising starkly out of the dust—that rival those of *Shane*, and are more effectively dramatic because they are less studied."

Not long after *From Hell to Texas*, Diane Varsi

made *Compulsion* (1959) with Orson Welles, then left movies. She walked out on her seven-year term contract with Fox and offered no explanation that made any sense when reporters hounded her at the Los Angeles airport as to why she would abandon such a promising film career for an unknown future in far-away Vermont. "I just want to be left alone," Varsi said, adding that she was confused about her meteoric rise in Hollywood. "Acting is destructive to me. I don't see any reason to be made miserable just because other people say I should go on with my career."

As it happened, the "married woman" whom Don Murray mentioned was having an affair with Dennis Hopper while shooting *From Hell to Texas* was his co-star, Diane Varsi. R. G. Armstrong remembered that Hopper persuaded Varsi to side with him in battles against Hathaway.

"Diane Varsi was a very unusual girl, very much like the character in the film," Don Murray explained. "She was kind of outspoken; she was introverted and her own person. Then she just left acting all together, and I think she became a librarian or something back east. Then later on she did a comeback film with me, a very different film than this. It was called *Sweet Love, Bitter* (1967), with Dick Gregory, a race-relations film about Charlie Parker, the jazz legend. But her film career really didn't flourish, and she died very young. So it was a shame."

There was one other *From Hell to Texas* reunion worth mentioning. Dennis Hopper *did* work again in Hollywood after all, and twice more with Henry Hathaway in fact! The unconventional Hopper (he was a Republican) claimed he *was* blackballed by Hollywood, thanks to Hathaway, but *did* continue acting, initially in TV, then eventually before movie cameras again. He directed and co-starred in the counterculture classic *Easy Rider* (1969), which made him rich and altered the Hollywood landscape. In fact, Hopper enjoyed a long and prolific acting, writing, and directing career. Even Hathaway asked Hopper to work with him again, on two big John Wayne films, *The Sons of Katie Elder* (1965) and *True Grit* (1969). According to Hopper, the reason for this was that he had married "a nice Irish woman," Brooke Hayward, favored by Wayne and Hathaway. She was the daughter of producer-agent Leland Hayward and actress Margaret Sullavan.

At last older and wiser, Hopper told a reporter,

"Hathaway would give you directions for very strange, uncomfortable movements. But he had everybody moving like that, so if you weren't doing that, you were in another movie. Now I realize he seldom dollies his camera. He goes from one still shot to another. It's the style of [Howard] Hawks and others. You begin to realize that what he's doing is getting *you* to move because his camera doesn't move. It's the simplest way to make movies and often a good way. You shouldn't overcomplicate the medium.

"Hathaway taught me a great lesson, a lesson I don't think I was able to accept until that point in my life, but one I've never forgotten. Don't fool with the director! He's the man in charge, and he gets what he wants. Just imagine what a mixture of styles and effects you would get if everyone was doing his own thing as an actor in a movie—what confusion! I love Henry now. There's nothing I wouldn't do for him." At Hathaway's funeral in 1985 his widow told Hopper, "Henry loved you so much and talked about you all the time." For his part, the actor later declared, "I learned more from him than from any other director."

The box-office failure of *From Hell to Texas* did not appreciably harm Don Murray's career. Although he had proven more than capable in the role, the erstwhile Actor's Studio thespian was neither suited nor inclined to star in Westerns or outdoor-action films. His natural sensitivity and intellectual curiosity showed to much better advantage in such films as the aforementioned *Hoodlum Priest* and *Advise and Consent*. Although he continued to play the occasional Westerner—such as Wild Bill Hickok in the 1966 remake of Cecil B. De Mille's *The Plainsman*—Murray wisely pursued variety in his roles and satisfied himself with meaty character parts when leads weren't available to him. He attained cult status with appearances in *Conquest of the Planet of the Apes* (1972) and the primetime TV soap opera *Knots Landing* (1979-81). A true gentleman with a keen, analytical mind, Murray has accomplished much during a show-business career now in its seventh decade. Yet his obvious affection for Lone Pine's natural beauty and wistful nostalgia for the days of *From Hell to Texas* still comes through, and it made him one of the most popular guests our annual Film Festival has ever welcomed. □□□

THE RANOWN TRIO

Three late Randolph Scott starrers,
written by Burt Kennedy and directed by Budd Boetticher,
rank among the best Westerns filmed in Lone Pine.

by Ed Hulse

Among the many movie cowboys associated with Lone Pine films, few enjoyed such lengthy careers as Randolph Scott, who first roamed the Alabama Hills in 1933 but is best remembered for Westerns he made there a quarter century later. Nearing the end of his long tenure as a horse-opera star, Scott teamed with producer Harry Joe Brown, screenwriter Burt Kennedy, and director Budd Boetticher to turn out several back-to-back genre classics that are even more highly regarded today than they were during their original theatrical playoffs.

Even in his earliest screen roles, Scott exuded the charm of a courtly Southern gentleman. This was no affectation but, rather, who he was at his core. The scion of a well-to-do family, George Randolph Scott was born on January 23, 1898. His birthplace is given as Orange County, Virginia, but he was raised in Charlotte, North Carolina, the second oldest of six siblings. Young "Randy" attended private schools, getting good grades and also distinguishing himself in competitive football, baseball, and swimming. Although he qualified for college on both financial and scholastic grounds, Scott in 1917 enlisted in the U. S. Army as a 19-year-old, serving in France with the 19th Field Artillery unit.

After the Armistice of November 11, 1918, Randy returned home and continued his education, first at Georgia Tech and then at the University of North Carolina. He was well on his way to becoming an All-American football player when a back injury sidelined him. Subsequently Scott dropped out of college and went to work as an accountant in his father's textile firm. Several years later he developed an interest in acting and decided to go west in search of motion-picture opportunities. His father reportedly penned a letter of introduction that Randy presented to young Howard Hughes, to whom the elder Scott had a business-related connection. Several sources indicate that Hughes helped procure for the wannabe actor a bit part in the 1928 George O'Brien starrer *Sharp Shooters*, but as Hughes was not affiliated with the Fox Film Corporation (which produced and distributed the film), the validity of this claim has been called into question. Scott *is* visible in *Sharp Shooters*, a late-silent comedy that has been preserved by the UCLA Film & Television Archive, but to the extent to which Hughes was responsible for his casting has yet to be determined.

In any event, Scott made the rounds in Hollywood and secured bit parts in other films, including Gary Cooper's 1929 version of *The Virginian*. He also did stage work at the famed Pasadena Playhouse and eventually attracted the attention of a casting director at Adolph Zukor's Paramount Publix Corporation, which signed him to a seven-year contract in 1932. The studio lost no time getting its new discovery in front of a camera, trying him out

Randolph Scott as he looked in the late 1940s, around the time he partnered with Harry Joe Brown.

with a minor role in *Sky Bride*, a star vehicle for fan favorite Richard Arlen.

Zukor had a long-standing arrangement with phenomenally popular Western writer Zane Grey, whose best-selling books were typically adapted by the studio shortly after appearing in print. (An early group of Grey novels was tied up by Fox owing to a long-term deal signed in 1918, but Paramount corralled screen rights to most of the others.) Given that these properties had a built-in following—the author's readers numbered in the millions—Zukor used the Zane Grey Westerns to showcase new contract players. Gary Cooper, Richard Dix, William Powell, and Richard Arlen were just a few actors whose early Paramount pictures were Grey oaters. Tall, lanky, masculine Scott—a competent horseman and superb athlete—was a natural for these films, all of them shot in rugged, picturesque locations. His tyro entry in the long-running series was 1932's *Heritage of the Desert*, an adaptation of Grey's first successful yarn. He would go on to make nine more, including *The Thundering Herd* (1933), shot in Lone Pine.

Randy was not immediately typecast as a Western star. While at Paramount he also appeared in dramas (such as 1932's *Hot Saturday*, opposite long-time roommate Cary Grant), thrillers (1933's *Murders in the Zoo*, supporting Lionel Atwill), and comedies (1936's *Go West, Young Man*, as a paramour of Mae West). He proved surprisingly adept in sprightly non-musical roles in two Fred Astaire-Ginger Rogers movies, 1935's *Roberta* and 1936's *Follow the Fleet*, for which he was loaned to RKO Radio Pictures. But he never stayed out of the saddle for long.

After leaving Paramount to freelance, Scott continued to make Westerns, starring in some and sharing the spotlight in others. He didn't have the lead role in *Jesse James* (1939), but he played Wyatt Earp in *Frontier Marshal* the same year. He supported Errol Flynn in *Virginia City* (1940) and vied with Robert Young for the attention of Virginia Gilmore in *Western Union*, Fox's 1941 adaptation of Zane Grey's final novel. He was a memorable villain in Universal's 1942 version of Rex Beach's oft-filmed *The Spoilers*. The trajectory of his career was altered by *The Desperadoes* (1943), a big-budget horse opera that was also the first Technicolor film made by Columbia Pictures: The producer of

that opus was one Harry Joe Brown, with whom Scott would later partner. Their association began in 1947 with *Gunfighters*, yet another Zane Grey adaptation, and picked up steam the next year with *Coroner Creek*, which presaged the films they would make the following decade with Budd Boetticher and Burt Kennedy. Based on a suspenseful novel by Luke Short, it cast Scott as a grim, bitter Westerner determined to find and take revenge on the killer of his fiancée. *Coroner Creek* was tough—even brutal, in spots—and uncompromising, showing the generally amiable star in a harsh light. Not the sort of fare aimed at young Saturday-matinee audiences, it satisfied mature viewers and provided a virtual template for the later films that are the focus of this article.

At the same time he was making Westerns with Harry Joe Brown, Scott was starring in medium-budget oaters produced by Nat Holt and released by both RKO and Fox. He even made a handful shot at least partially in Lone Pine and/or the Eastern Sierras: *The Doolins of Oklahoma* (1949), *The Nevadan* (1950), *Man in the Saddle* (1951), *Hangman's Knot* (1952), and *The Stranger Wore a Gun* (1953). Cut to a conventional pattern, these increasingly similar movies had the unfortunate effect of diluting Scott's appeal. Over-exposed on the nation's theater screens, the star began slipping; He retained a faithful fan following but his box-office potency had been diminished considerably when in 1955 he was approached by former co-star John Wayne with a proposition.

Wayne's production company, Batjac, had recently received a Western script titled *Seven Men from Now* from first-time screenwriter Burt Kennedy. Batjac had a distribution deal with Warner Brothers and owed the studio one more picture. But the Duke was about to begin shooting *The Searchers* for his old mentor John Ford, and he had been persuaded to pass on Kennedy's script anyway. In the interest of fulfilling his commitment to Warners, however, Wayne suggested producing the picture economically and giving the lead role to a star commanding less money than he was getting. Duke knew that Scott's career was waning and suggested casting the lanky Southerner.

After reading the script and taking note of the proposed budget—substantially higher than those of

Scott with his partner and long-time producer, Harry Joe Brown, watching Brown's son taking aim with a slingshot.

Scott in *Seven Men from Now* (1956), the first of his Lone Pine films to be directed by Budd Boetticher.

his last few films—Scott agreed to star in *Seven Men from Now*. He was delighted with the choice of Budd Boetticher as director. A former assistant director whose lengthy apprenticeship included making "B" pictures for Columbia, Republic, and Monogram, Boetticher had first worked for the Duke's company, then called John Wayne Productions, in 1951. The ensuing picture, *Bullfighter and the Lady*, was beset with problems behind the scenes but indicated that its helmer showed great promise. According to some sources, Scott was already familiar with Boetticher's work when the two joined forces to make *Seven Men from Now* and, in fact, wanted Budd to join him and Harry Joe Brown.

The history of *Seven Men* has been exhaustively documented in a previous issue of *Lone Pine in the Movies*, but a few facts bear repeating. According to Burt Kennedy, during the first and only pre-production meeting in which John Wayne was personally involved—the first one with Scott and Boetticher in attendance—it was agreed that Lone Pine would be the primary location. Kennedy's plot called for Scott's character, a former sheriff, to become an avenging angel relentlessly trailing the seven men who killed his wife during a Wells Fargo holdup. The starkness of the story would be matched by the starkness of the location.

Boetticher staged sequences in the Alabama Hills but also in isolated spots north, south, east, and west of town. At 58 years of age Scott looked sufficiently weathered and world-weary to be supremely convincing as the vengeance-minded ex-lawman.

But then, he had the benefit of one of the best scripts yet written for him. In the aforementioned article film historian Packy Smith had this to say:

Most critics and film historians give Burt Kennedy's script the bulk of the credit for this movie's success. It is interesting to note that Boetticher, a man known for his huge ego and propensity to claim credit when it probably should have gone elsewhere, never tried to grab the glory that Kennedy earned by virtue of his superior screenplays. For his part, Kennedy always admitted that many of his rewrites were done after brainstorming with Boetticher and Scott to address specific problems. During production of all the Boetticher-Kennedy collaborations, Burt was on location and on set daily. He was quick to credit Boetticher with building suspense naturally and giving action sequences credible payoffs.

Seven Men from Now went into general release on August 4, 1956, eliciting favorable to enthusiastic reviews from critics who had given mediocre notices to Scott's last few pictures. The film racked up worldwide rentals of $1,690,000 on a negative cost of $719,000. Subtracting distribution fees and print costs, Warners realized a profit of $448,000.

Randolph Scott urged his partner, Harry Joe Brown, to sign both Boetticher and Kennedy to long-term contracts. The director had already been negotiating with Brown when *Seven Men* went before the cameras, but Burt was still under obligation to Batjac. Wayne's partner Robert Fellows became embroiled in a messy divorce, which forced him to sell his half of the company to Duke. The ensuing corporate shakeup freed Kennedy to join the Scott-Brown production unit, which also fell heir to one of Batjac's literary properties: a 1955 Elmore Leonard short story titled "The Captives," originally slated to be adapted by Kennedy, produced by Wayne's brother Bob Morrison, and directed by Andrew V. McLaglen.

Having arranged a distribution deal with Columbia Pictures, Scott and Brown decided to film "The Captives" under Leonard's title in the summer of 1956. They soon learned that another studio had registered the same title and changed their picture's name to *The Tall Rider*. Ultimately it went into release as *The Tall T*.

Elmore Leonard, best known today for his riveting crime yarns (many of them made into such popular movies and TV shows as *Justified*, *Jackie Brown*, and *Get Shorty*), began writing in the early Fifties, the waning days of the pulp-fiction era. He had an ear for crisp, naturalistic dialogue and developed a lean, unobtrusive prose style that made his stories particularly easy for scriptwriters to adapt. The "first act" of *Tall T* was devised by Burt Kennedy from a few lines of back-story, but the film's last two-thirds followed Leonard's original closely and incorporated virtually every line of dialogue used in it. The result was an unusually taut, suspenseful Western that remains a model of simple, direct big-screen storytelling.

The film opens with a glimpse of proud but struggling rancher Pat Brennan (played by Randolph Scott), heading for the town of Contention when he stops at a stage-line relay station to visit briefly with the manager, Hank Parker (Fred Sherman), and his young son Jeff (Christopher Olsen). Arriving in town, he witnesses some boorish behavior from newly married Willard Mims (John Hubbard), who is leaving with his bride Doretta (Maureen O'Sullivan) on their honeymoon in a hired coach driven by grizzled Ed Rintoon (Arthur Hunnicutt). The crusty old-timer doesn't bother to conceal his disdain for the fortune-hunting Willard, who is known to have married the mousy, plain-looking woman to get her wealthy father's money.

Brennan proceeds to the Tall T ranch, where he long worked for its owner, Tenvoorde (Robert Burton). Pat hopes to buy a bull from his former employer, who offers to give him the animal if Brennan can ride the bucking beast. If he loses, however, Tenvoorde will get his horse. And that's exactly what happens.

Later, trudging along the dusty trail home, Pat sees Rintoon's coach approaching and hitches a ride over Willard's objections. Upon reaching the relay station, they are accosted by three men who order them to drop their guns. These outlaws—ruthless but intelligent Frank Usher (Richard Boone), trigger-happy Chink (Henry Silva), and dull-witted Billy Jack (Skip Homeier)—have just murdered Parker and his son and dumped their bodies into the nearby well. Rintoon grabs for a rifle hidden in the stage's "boot" but is shot dead by Chink.

After Usher hints that he intends to murder the passengers, the cowardly Mims reveals that his new bride is the daughter of a wealthy copper miner and suggests that his father-in-law will happily pay a large ransom for the safe return of his daughter. Eager to get away, Mims even volunteers to deliver the ransom note himself. Usher writes a note demanding $50,000 and instructs Billy Jack to accompany the cowardly husband and rejoin them later at their hideout in the hills, where Pat and Doretta will be held prisoner.

That night, the two captives are forced into a crude lean-to built over a shallow hillside cave, while Usher and Chink remain on guard outside by a fire. Unaware that her husband has betrayed her, Doretta naïvely proclaims her faith in Mims, and Brennan—realizing how desperate their plight is—says nothing to disabuse her of that comforting notion.

The following morning, Usher voices grudging respect for Brennan and tries to engage him in friendly conversation. He admits caring little for the company of Chink and Billy Jack. The rancher senses that his only opportunity for survival may rest on driving a wedge between the three outlaws.

Billy Jack and Willard arrive and report that Doretta's father has agreed to deliver the ransom money the next morning. Mims asks permission to leave and is willing to do so without even saying goodbye to his frightened wife. Disgusted by the man, Usher shoos Willard away but orders Chink to shoot him in the back. Then the bandit leader heartlessly breaks the news to Doretta that her husband betrayed her. That night in the lean-to, she admits to Pat that she suspected Willard never loved her, but married the man anyway out of loneliness and desperation. Brennan shuts down this pity party and roughly kisses the recently minted widow to assure her that she has the making of a desirable woman.

The next morning, Usher rides out to collect the ransom at the agreed-upon location, leaving Chink and Billy Jack behind. With this opportunity to foment suspicion, Pat hints to the two gunmen that their boss plans to double-cross them. When Chink takes the bait and rides off to find Usher, Brennan instructs the woman to lure the sexually inexperienced Billy Jack into the lean-to. When the young bandit seizes Doretta, Pat charges him and a struggle for Billy Jack's gun ensues. The outlaw is killed and Chink, not yet far away, rides back to camp after hearing gunfire. Now armed, Pat brings Doretta into the rocks and hides there, then engages the returning Chink and eventually guns him down.

Shortly thereafter, Usher returns to camp with the ransom money and discovers the bodies of his hapless partners. Brennan gets the drop on the bandit chief, who cleverly plays on Pat's code of honor and persuades the rancher to let him ride away. Usher gets several hundred yards away before pulling his rifle from the saddle scabbard and riding back to shoot Pat, whose guard is down. But Brennan reacts quickly and unloads a shotgun blast in Usher's face. Doretta watches in horror as her kidnapper falls from his horse and, blinded and pain-maddened, staggers around the campsite before collapsing, dead. Sickened but relieved, Pat puts a comforting arm around Doretta and they head for the trail.

Film historian Sean Axmaker queried director Budd Boetticher about his Randolph Scott Westerns at great length during a series of wide-ranging interviews conducted between 1988 and 1992. Boetticher confirmed that he was the first and only choice to direct *The Tall T* once the property had been obtained from Batjac. "Harry Joe Brown [contacted me] because of Randy. Randy said, "I don't want anyone else to direct this." So they came and said, "Will you make another picture with Randolph Scott?" and I said, "I'd love it!" Thus was extended the successful star-director-writer collaboration that began with *Seven Men from Now*.

Kennedy and Boetticher worked on the *Tall T* script together, although, as previously mentioned, the latter two-thirds of the film utilized Elmore Leonard's original story practically word for word. Most of their effort was directed at establishing Scott's character and giving him a revenge motive by showing his friendship with the relay-station manager and his young son, who are callously murdered by the Usher gang.

There was no question but that the film would be shot in Lone Pine, and Kennedy's script was crafted in such a way to avoid the need for potentially costly interior sets. The only actual set was the hillside cave, which was small and easily constructed. The Alabama Hills would provide ample production value, and their stark beauty provided a fitting backdrop to the harsh, gritty elements in Kennedy's script.

0 CPC-8379-78

Randolph Scott as rancher Pat Brennan in *The Tall T* (1957), which reunited him with Boetticher and Kennedy.

Pat Brennan (Scott) and Ed Rintoon (Arthur Hunnicutt) are headed for trouble, but they don't know it yet.

Brennan and Rintoon meet in town before the latter begins his ill-fated coach ride with newlyweds Willard and Doretta Mims.

Of course, there were a few pre-production holdups. One of them involved the casting of Frank Usher. Boetticher originally had *Seven Men from Now* player Lee Marvin in mind for the role but found the actor unavailable, as he explained to Sean Axmaker:

I needed somebody to take the place of Lee Marvin, who suddenly was a big star. I had seen Richard Boone with the wonderful pockmarked face, and I begin watching *Medic* [a 1954-56 TV series starring Boone]. And the studio head said to me, "You don't want to use him." I said, "Why?" And he said, "Well, you know, he has no sense of humor. Your stuff is funny." And I said, "Well, I bet he does." And he says, "Well, look, you're going to get what you want anyway. But do Columbia Pictures a favor: Have him over to lunch, go to dinner with him, spend some time with him. See what he's really like. Please don't just go out and hire him." And so I said, "Okay, I will."

So I called him and I said, "Mr. Boone, this is Budd Boetticher." And he said, "Oh, congratulations. I just saw *Seven Men from Now*." And I said, "Well, we can do the same thing with you, but I have a little bit of a problem. Can you come in today and have lunch with me and maybe spend the rest of the day, and we'll get to know each other? It's at the request of the studio." And he said, "What seems to be the trouble?" And I said, "Well, I really don't want to tell you yet." But he said, "I can't do it, Budd, my wife maybe has cancer." (But fortunately, she didn't). And he said, "We're on the way this afternoon to Scripps Clinic near San Diego, and I won't be back until the end of the week. What really is the trouble?" And I said, "Well, the heads of the studio don't think you have a sense of humor." He said, "Well, you've got to admit those heart operations [in *Medic*] are pretty friggin' funny." So I said, "Don't even bother to come in to lunch. Just go to wardrobe and we'll get you in." And that was Richard Boone.

Boone was, in fact, quick to laugh, and his unplanned reaction to a blooper was left in the film, as Boetticher explained:

In *The Tall T*, remember when Randy comes out of the hut and hits his head? That was an accident. Then I made Boone laugh and it's very funny and people love it. But Randy came out and he's, you know, six foot four and he really banged his head and what we didn't save was the [take] when he was really groggy. He comes out and hits his head and I cut to Richard Boone and he started to laugh and it worked.

Like all good directors, Boetticher brought all his life experiences to bear when helming a production. Budd called on his knowledge of bullfighting—which had informed his first personal project, *Bullfighter and the Lady* (1951), made for John Wayne's production unit headquartered at Republic Pictures—when staging Pat Brennan's abortive bull ride at the Tall T ranch owned by Tenvoorde. He explained the situation to Axmaker:

I know that a bull doesn't like water. The way they found this out, years ago, the first bullrings in the world were really informal bullrings, what we call the *zocalo* in Mexico. They were public circles in Spain where eight or ten or six or five streets ran in and in the middle of that enclosure, which now they've blocked off with bales of hay and carts and things and the front row seats in 1800 were the balconies in the homes surrounding the circle, always in the middle was a fountain and when the bullfighters got in real trouble, and I've been in that position, and the bull hooked your cape or *muleta* out of the way, you dive into the fountain. The bull didn't want to go in there. That's why the Brahma bull is in *The Tall T*. The stunt man came to me and I said, "All you have to do, and the bull's gonna come after you, all you have to do is dive in there and go to the bottom of the water trough." He said, "Are you kidding?" I said, "No, he's not going to get you." And he didn't and it was wonderful. [The stunt man] didn't believe it. The bull even stepped in after him and suddenly got his nose wet and thought, "I don't want to drown." And those are the things that you use with experience in other things.

It was actually one of the two-legged performers that gave Boetticher more trouble than the Brahma bull:

I had Arthur Hunnicutt, who was so drunk during the filming of the opening of *The Tall T* that we did that dolly shot across the street with Randy 28 times. Next time you see it, look at Randy's face. He's trying not to laugh because Arthur Hunnicutt is ad-libbing. And we couldn't find any liquor, we couldn't find where the hell he was getting a drink. One of my assistants, Joe Kenny, suddenly realized that he was sucking on oranges all day long,

Frank Usher (Richard Boone, left) orders henchman Chink (Henry Silva) to watch Mrs. Mims (Maureen O'Sullivan).

and we discovered what he would do. He would take a hypodermic needle and fill the oranges full of vodka. You have things like that and you go absolutely crazy, because drunks are brilliant. Talk about hiding your bottle, like in *The Lost Weekend* in the chandelier and forgetting where you put it, these guys, to get a drink, they're amazing.

Boetticher, cinematographer Charles Lawton Jr., and assistant director Sam Nelson wisely selected locations in advance to facilitate rapid shooting on a short schedule. The sequence at Tenvoorde's ranch was shot in a corral that still stands today, more than a half century later. Lush meadows east of the Alabams on Russ Spainhower's Anchor Ranch saw some action, as did Movie Road, along which Brennan trudges on foot, saddle slung over his shoulder, before hailing Rintoon's coach.

Randolph Scott's previously tarnished reputation had some of its luster restored following the critical and commercial success of *Seven Men from Now*. *The Tall T*, while not quite as profitable, elicited equally enthusiastic notices and undoubtedly helped

extend Scott's career. It was followed by *Decision at Sundown* (1957) and *Buchanan Rides Alone* (1958), also directed by Boetticher but scripted by Charles Lang, a veteran "B"-movie scribe who lacked Kennedy's panache. The difference in their output was not lost on Budd:

[*Decision and Buchanan*] were very different and they weren't as good. And they were too complicated. In *Decision at Sundown*, [Scott's character] had mental problems that he really didn't have in Burt's pictures. It was a picture that [Scott and Brown] had bought. It wasn't a Randolph Scott character. It was the story of a town, the story of a lot of people. It was like … the old-fashioned Randolph Scott picture, it wasn't one man who had a job to do, who had a problem to overcome. It wasn't the kind of pictures that Burt and I made together. The scripts weren't as good.

[On the script of *Buchanan Rides Alone*:] Charlie Lang was under tremendous pressure and I knew that I had the ability to fix it. He was going through a divorce, a very sad divorce. I went to Mexico and left Charlie the treatment

Beautifully composed and lit shot of Pat and Doretta taking cover after making their escape from Billy Jack.

Brennan is prepared to give Usher just one chance for his life, and if the outlaw is smart he'll take it.

Another stunning portrait of Scott framed against the Sierras, this one from *Ride Lonesome* (1959).

Bounty hunter Ben Brigade (Scott) captures killer Billy John (James Best) in *Ride Lonesome*.

that we had written, called *The Name's Buchanan*. I was late in coming home and I drove directly from Mexico City to Tucson and I got there four or five days before the picture was to start. [Cinematographer] Lucien [Ballard] was supposed to get there the day before the picture was to start and he walked into breakfast four days before and threw the script at me. He said, "Have you read this?" I said, "What do you mean *read* it? I *wrote* it." He said, "You didn't write this piece of shit."

I started to read it, and with all the tension that Charlie was under, he had made that script as if we had given him a baseball picture and all of the sudden we were doing an underwater film. I mean, it was completely different than the stuff that we had given him. But, he made his money, he's a great, great friend of mine now and you just have to understand these things. A lot of people get drunk when they have a situation like that and can't work and Charlie

just wasn't paying attention to what he was supposed to do. His loyalty to me was to write a script and he wrote one, but he didn't read the one we gave him. So that's what happened there. And I called Burt and said "Burt, we're really in trouble," so we ad-libbed the whole damn thing. The only way that that script got into script form was the script clerk, the script girl would write down what we *did*, not what we were *going* to do.

Decision at Sundown and *Buchanan Rides Alone* were clearly not in the same league as *Seven Men from Now* and *The Tall T*, but they weren't embarrassments, nor did they lose money. Yet Randolph Scott and Harry Joe Brown must have suspected that more pictures like them could slow the aging star's newly accelerating career momentum. Worse yet, Scott owed one more

RANDOLPH SCOTT
DCPC-8506-45

Here's one more portrait of Randolph Scott taken during the production of *Ride Lonesome*.

Ben Brigade is really just using Billy John as bait to lure the young killer's brother Frank.

picture to Warner Brothers—one over which he had no control. Berne Giler's screenplay was depressingly routine and Scott begged producer Henry Blanke to let Boetticher direct. The film, released as *Westbound* (1959), added no laurels to either man's career. Budd later referred to it as "a rescue mission" designed to extricate Scott from his Warners commitment as painlessly as possible.

The Scott-Brown production unit, operating as Ranown Pictures Corporation, still had its berth at Columbia, but top studio executives fretted that Harry Joe Brown, nearing 70 years of age, was no longer up to the task. He began making mistakes, some of them costly. Yet the entire unit knew that the accumulated experience of this silent-era veteran was still invaluable, and everybody from Scott and Boetticher on down resorted to subterfuge to save the old man's job. The director was approached to take over the "line producing" of Scott's Westerns.

When Sean Axmaker asked him why, the still-loyal Budd explained it thusly:

Harry Joe Brown was a darling guy ... I'll tell you a very funny story about him. When we were making *Buchanan* we were supposed to finish on Friday at four o'clock in the afternoon, and on Thursday I was filming around two o'clock in the afternoon, and I had about 250 servicemen and their wives and children on the set, and we were working our tails off on the bridge, and we were really ad-libbing the picture. Harry Joe Brown came running up to me and said, "When are you going to finish?" I said, "About four or five o'clock." He said "Today?" I said "Hell no, tomorrow, like we're supposed to." He said, "You've gotta finish today. I made a mistake, the airplane is here." And you asked me why I wanted to produce the last pictures? Can you imagine?

So I said, "Harry Joe, what I think we ought to do is, we'll finish tomorrow and check everybody out of the hotels at

Ben Brigade has become the reluctant protector of Carrie Lane (Karen Steele), wife of the missing stationmaster suspected by being killed by Indians.

Showdown time! Brigade leads Billy John to the hanging tree while Whit (James Coburn) and Carrie watch nervously for Frank's arrival.

JCPCB506·14

night, and we'll sleep in our seats on the plane tonight." I mean it was terrible, what a mistake. Here's this big DC-4 sitting at the airport and we've got another 48 hours to go. But Harry Joe, because he was such an ambitious guy … would go out and put everybody in the wrong costumes and shoot second units. So Randy would come riding over the hill in a red shirt and we'd cut back to the close-up and he's in black.

I didn't want anybody screwing around with these [next] two pictures, so Harry Joe was executive producer and he had two things that he could do: He could come on the set and tell me the rushes were great, or he could have a cup of coffee. That wasn't being tough, because I really loved him. Columbia wanted to cut him out completely. That's how tough the studio is: "You don't need Harry Joe Brown." We said, "Harry Joe Brown has given you the better part of his life at Columbia, of *course* you need Harry Joe Brown." They said, "Well what's he going to do?" We said, "He's the executive producer and he's going to get his same salary and I'll produce the picture."

We didn't change a thing because we had done the same thing on all the other pictures, all of a sudden my name was up there as producer. No, I never produced the pictures. Harry Joe did the job but I still made the pictures with Burt and with Randy and Harry Joe gave us what we wanted. A producer should help you get the cast, he should make you suggestions about the script, he should handle the financing so that you get enough of what you need. But we didn't have any official bothering or second units during lunch or problems.

Burt Kennedy had written an original screenplay titled *Ride Lonesome*, which became the next Ranown production. It sported a deceptively simple yet compelling plot that, like *Tall T,* was populated with a small group of principal characters around whose interactions the film revolves.

Bounty hunter Ben Brigade (Scott) finds his man, a heartless young killer named Billy John (James Best), camped on a rocky ridge in high-desert country. He announces his intention of returning Billy to the town of Santa Cruz for hanging. Brigade is nearly ambushed by one of Billy's friends hiding in the rocks above, but warns the would-be bushwhacker that he'll kill the prisoner then and there if shot at again. Billy hollers at his cohort, urging him to tell the killer's older brother, Frank (Lee Van Cleef), that he's been captured and is being taken to Santa Cruz.

The hidden assailant emerges from the rocks and rides away, hell bent for leather.

En route, Brigade and his prisoner come upon a stage-line way station that seems deserted. As they approach, an outlaw named Sam Boone (Pernell Roberts) hails the bounty hunter, with whom he is acquainted. Carrie Lane (Karen Steele), wife of the absent station master, has been hiding from Boone and his partner Whit (James Coburn), but she takes advantage of Brigade's arrival to reveal herself. Brandishing a shotgun, she orders all four men to leave. Just then a stagecoach barrels down the trail toward the station at breakneck speed. Only after the horses crash into the corral do Brigade and the others see that the driver is dead, an Indian spear through his chest. A quick examination of the coach shows that the passengers too have been killed.

The bounty hunter suspects that Boone and Whit planned to rob the stage but forms an alliance with them for the duration of the Indian siege he

RANDOLPH SCOTT
© CPC-8506-46

Randolph Scott as Ben Brigade, ready for action in the Alabama Hills as *Ride Lonesome* unfolds.

Jefferson Cody (Scott) barters with Indians for a white woman in *Comanche Station* (1960).

believes to be imminent. Boone explains to Brigade that he and Whit are really interested in Billy John: Total amnesty has been promised to anybody who returns the killer to Santa Cruz, and the two small-time outlaws are determined to have their slates cleaned so they can begin working the ranch Boone has purchased in anticipation of going straight. Paradoxically, they are prepared to take Billy by force, even if it means killing Brigade.

A band of Indians suddenly appears on the horizon and offers to negotiate with the bounty hunter, who speaks their language. Brigade speaks with the chief and reports to the others that the Indian wants Carrie for his squaw and has offered to trade a horse for her. The woman shrieks when she recognizes the horse—it belonged to her husband,

who has obviously been killed by the savages. The braves scatter but reappear a short time later to attack the party of whites, now riding toward Santa Cruz. Brigade and the others take cover in an adobe shack and fight off the Indians, killing the chief.

Meanwhile, Billy John's brother Frank and his men reach the way station and discover tracks indicating that people have recently left. He follows the tracks.

Not eager to swap lead with the much-feared Frank, Whit tries persuading Boone to abandon his plan. But the latter has his mind set on winning amnesty, even if it means gunning Brigade down. He actually likes and respects the bounty hunter, but Billy stands between them and Boone's passport to a new life. Nonetheless, he saves Brigade from the prisoner when Billy craftily manages to seize a rifle

Cody has rescued Nancy Lowe (Nancy Gates), whose husband is offering a reward for her return.

and points it at his captor's belly. And he even offers to pay the bounty on Billy's head if the bounty hunter will hand him over. But Brigade refuses to surrender the killer and warns Boone against trying to take the kid by force.

The fact that Billy's captor has made no effort to cover his tracks perplexes Frank until he realizes that Brigade is only using the young man as bait to lure his older brother into a trap. Frank explains to one of his men that he once did the bounty hunter wrong. It develops that the notorious badman killed Brigade's wife by hanging her from a tree.

A day's ride outside Santa Cruz, the bounty hunter and his party reach the clearing where that fateful tree still stands. After they make camp at a riverbed nearby, Brigade finally explains his game: When he was sheriff of Santa Cruz, he arrested Frank for murder. The miscreant broke jail, kidnapped Brigade's wife, and hanged her from the tree. The erstwhile star-packer resigned, became a bounty hunter, and rode a solitary trail, biding his time until a way of revenging himself on Frank presented itself. When Billy committed murder and had a price put on his head, Brigade saw his chance and took it. He well knows that the killer's older brother is right behind them—and that the day of reckoning has arrived.

Understanding Brigade's motive, Boone offers to cover the ex-sheriff when he confronts Frank, who arrives in short order. Brigade leads Billy to the hanging tree, puts a noose around the boy's neck, and dares Frank to stop the hanging. The outlaw charges with guns blazing and Brigade downs him easily while Boone and Whit make short work of the gang. His mission completed, Brigade turns Billy over to Boone and Whit. The others head for Santa Cruz, but the bounty hunter stays behind just long enough to set the hanging tree on fire.

With the exception of *Seven Men from Now*, *Ride Lonesome* is the best of the Scott-Boetticher-Kennedy collaborations. The story is basically just an extended chase, the cast has only six principals and a handful of bit players, and the entire movie unfolds outdoors. But its 73 minutes are intensely suspenseful and satisfying, and as a Lone Pine movie *Ride Lonesome* is hard to beat. The Alabama Hills make their first appearance underneath the opening credits in a slow tracking shot that follows Scott as

he heads up the winding trail to the ridge where Billy John is camped. Once again, Boetticher's mastery of composition is evident in his groupings of the main characters in the anamorphic frame. Charles Lawton Jr.'s cinematography, too, is first-rate, especially in the day-for-night scenes he captures through a filtered lens. The sand dunes outside of Olancha, to the south of Lone Pine, are employed to good effect, as are the meadows on the Anchor Ranch.

The relationship between Scott's character and those played by Roberts and Coburn is one of the most interesting in Western-movie history. Kennedy's script makes clear in no uncertain terms that the two outlaws have unsavory pasts, and that the bounty hunter is familiar with their depredations from his days as the sheriff of Santa Cruz. Nonetheless, they remain calm and cordial, even when a deadly confrontation seems to be the only way out of their respective dilemmas. Equally interesting is the interaction of Sam Boone with his simple-minded but amiable partner Whit. Boetticher came to like these characters a great deal as filming progressed and ordered script changes to beef up the roles— with Scott's approval. As the director later explained the situation:

Pernell Roberts and James Coburn were to be killed. And I called the studio [production chief] Sam Briskin and said, "Sam, I don't want to kill these guys." It's halfway through the picture. And he said, "Well, you have to, they're the villains." I said, "No, I don't have to, they're charming, the people are going to love them." Especially after the scene that Coburn says to [Roberts] about the friendship: "Gee, I didn't know that." I mean, you love this simple guy, and that was Jim's first picture and look what happened with him. And of course Pernell went right into his big series [*Bonanza*] and nobody was more charming than Pernell was. So I argued and argued and argued…. I said "Sam, I'll shoot it both ways. I'll shoot it where they go free, and we'll ad lib the ending," which we did, "and I'll shoot it when we kill them." Well, the darnedest thing happened. We had arranged, because the sun was going down, for all the transportation to be ready. Just by sheer accident, it happened to be in the way where we wanted to shoot. It was the last day of filming and it took them about two hours to get all the transportation, the busses and the trucks, moved. By that time the sun had gone down and we never got to do [the killing of the two outlaws]. So I

The Comanches are on the warpath and have Cody and his party pinned down.

took it back to the studio having failed to shoot the death scene and they liked what we did so much that they didn't argue about it.

The final Ranown film was *Comanche Station* (1960), which reunited Scott with Boetticher and Kennedy for the last time.

A lone trader named Jefferson Cody (Scott) enters rugged Comanche country to barter for the freedom of a white woman taken prisoner by the savage Indians. He is successful and, after riding away with the woman, learns that she is Nancy Lowe (Nancy Gates), wife of a prominent Lordsburg citizen who has offered a $5000 reward for anyone who can return her to him. Cody says he rescued her simply because he heard that the Comanche were holding a white woman. Mrs. Lowe hints that she has been sexually abused by the Indians and asks the trader if

a husband would still want a wife who had been thus victimized. Cody replies that a man would take her back if he loved her enough.

They have just reached a stage-line outpost known as Comanche Station when three men ride in, hotly pursued by Indians. After helping the trio drive off the braves, Cody recognizes one of them as bounty hunter Ben Lane (Claude Akins), whom he had court-martialed for inciting Indians when both served in the Army years earlier. Cody suspects Lane and his companions, Dobie (Richard Rust) and Frank (Skip Homeier), of being caught collecting Comanche scalps, but the bounty hunter assures him that they have only been searching for Mrs. Lowe.

That night, while awaiting the arrival of the stage, Cody tells the woman he knew nothing about the reward, but she refuses to believe him. Lane warns Frank and Dobie to keep their eyes on the woman

Cody foils an attempt by renegade Ben Lane (Claude Akins) to get the drop on him.

and the taciturn trader: Since Lowe has offered to pay the reward whether his wife is returned dead or alive, the bounty hunter figures on killing both her and Cody to claim the money.

Morning brings an unwelcome surprise in the person of the mortally wounded stationmaster, who gasps out the news that Comanches are on the warpath and have massacred the stage driver and passengers. Cody realizes the group will have to make Lordsburg on horseback—and cooperate with each other in order to survive. While stopping at the river to rest, Frank is killed by an arrow. His friend Dobie, who has come to resent Lane, is tempted to chuck the murder plot when Cody offers to take the young man under his wing. Later, Dobie explains to Mrs. Lowe that Cody has spent years in Comanche country, looking for his own wife who was kidnapped by Indians.

While riding ahead of the party to scout for Comanche raiders, Cody is attacked by braves and rescued by Lane, who can't bear to see another white man murdered by the savages. Despite this apparently selfless act, the trader realizes that he can't trust Lane and Dobie, disarms them, and drives them away at gunpoint as the party approaches Lordsburg. Having hidden a rifle, the bounty hunter ride ahead and lays in wait to ambush Cody and the woman when they ride past. Dobie tries to prevent and is shot for his trouble. But the sound of gunfire tips Cody off, and after urging Mrs. Lowe to take cover he kills Lane before the latter can gun her down.

During the dangerous journey Cody has wondered what kind of man is willing to pay others to rescue his woman. Upon returning Mrs. Lowe to her home, he finds out: When her husband and their son come out of the house to welcome her, Cody see that the

Jefferson Cody is not a man to be trifled with, as his adversaries are about to learn.

man is blind and therefore obviously unable to search for his wife. Mrs. Lowe thanks Cody, who refuses the reward and rides away—back to the rugged hills of Comanche territory, where we first saw him, to resume the quest for his own wife.

Comanche Station is bookended by identical sequences that call to mind that clichéd phrase "poetry in motion." They are simple pan shots following a solitary rider, Jefferson Cody, as he slowly ascends a trail into the hills—a man on a quest, a man with a mission. As the movie begins he probably believes he's found the missing wife for whom he's searched so long. As it ends, following the return of a grateful Mrs. Lowe to her home and family, Cody begins his search anew, theoretically hoping that this trip will be his last, the one that reunites him with his lost love. Film buffs aware that *Station* is Scott's final solo starring vehicle can be forgiven for investing that final sequence with a little extra poignancy.

With *Comanche Station* the remarkable collaboration of Randolph Scott, Budd Boetticher, and Burt Kennedy came to an end. The latter two continued working for many years, but Scott made just one more movie, Sam Peckinpah's elegiac *Ride the High Country*, before retiring in 1962. A phenomenally wealthy man—he collected oil wells the way some boys collect baseball cards—Scott enjoyed his retirement and lived another quarter-century, dying in 1987 at the ripe old age of 89.

In one of his interviews with Sean Axmaker, the director summed up his experience with the Scott-Brown unit:

Burt and Randy and Harry Joe and I had complete control and we all thought alike. It was a pleasure because I had the best cameramen, who were my friends, and I had a producer I really liked because he didn't bother me, Harry Joe Brown, and I don't think there was ever a finer

Cody gives Mrs. Lane a six-gun and tells her to stay under cover during the coming shootout.

gentleman in the picture business than Randolph Scott. And where John Wayne had a completely different attitude with young actors who were in his pictures, Randy would say "I sure like that young fellow," like James Coburn, "let's give him more 'lyrics' [lines of dialogue]." In every picture I made with him, with the exception of *Westbound*, we made a star because Randy and Burt and I wanted to make a star. And look at the list: Lee Marvin, Richard Boone, Craig Stevens, Pernell Roberts, James Coburn, Claude Akins. Every picture. I mean I could write a whole book just about Randolph Scott. But everybody felt that way about him. Burt wrote five of the seven screenplays, and he was a great, great, writer and is a wonderful director and one of my dearest friends. We wrote and directed as two great friends who work together instead of a writer and director who didn't get along and trying to take control of the picture. It was just a difference, we had artistic control and fortunately we were artists. A very simple answer why they were better pictures….

I don't think we ever had an argument in all those pictures. If [Scott] thought I was wrong about something he would just be very quiet and walk away and I would wonder what was the matter, and I was so fond of him that I'd say, "Wait a minute, let's try—Randy, do you have an idea on this?" "Well, I thought maybe that if we did this and this …." And he was usually right about it. But usually it only pertained to what he thought about his character. He never said, "I think that Richard Boone should say this and do that." He never did that. He'd say, "I think that maybe if I stop there as if I was gonna take a drink and then I'd change my mind, there might be a little beat in there that …." I'd say, "That's great. Let's do it."

Of his favorite location (and ours), Boetticher had this to say:

I probably shot in Lone Pine in color more than anybody. They used to make pictures there in black and white, Roy Rogers films and stuff like that. You had everything there. You had rivers on one side of the road to San Francisco, you had mountains on the other, you had rocks, you had desert, everything. Can you imagine? The desert in *Ride Lonesome* was 15 minutes from those rocks, just on the other side of the road. They call them the Alabams. You can't lose that way. When you make a picture in 18 days, which everybody should be taught to do, you don't have time to fool around and get in an airplane and go to another city.

In his essay "What Randolph Scott Knew," drama critic and popular culture commentator Terry Teachout expressed great fondness for the Lone Pine-shot Ranown pictures, which he likened to the work of master artists:

Just as Degas never tired of the ballet dancers he painted time and again, so does Boetticher come up with ever-fresh ways to frame his players among the sun-scorched rocks of Lone Pine, finding painfully austere beauty in that least seductive of landscapes. Though he was never obvious about it, Boetticher was among the most visually imaginative of Western directors. I once had the opportunity to ask him if his feel for composition had been shaped by the paintings of such artists as Albert Bierstadt and Frederic Remington, to which he replied that while he liked their work, Renoir and Toulouse-Lautrec had meant even more to him. (I could see how much he enjoyed telling me that, too.)

Teachout's admiration extended to the scripts as well:

Similarly, Burt Kennedy makes a virtue out of necessity by letting Scott and his engaging enemies spend most of their time talking instead of fighting. He gives the best lines to the not-entirely-bad-guys—Lee Marvin in *Seven Men from Now*, Richard Boone in *The Tall T*, Pernell Roberts in *Ride Lonesome*, Claude Akins in Comanche Station—and it is Roberts, not Scott, who gets the line that could stand as the motto of all six films, "There are some things a man just can't ride around."

Scott was secure enough to let his colleagues do the talking, knowing that his gritty, hard-faced on-screen presence would speak for itself. The dashing young leading man of the Thirties now looked as though he'd been carved from a stump, and every word he spoke reeked of disillusion. Yet he continually found himself forced to make moral choices that were always clear but rarely easy. What Scott should do at any given moment is never in doubt, but we also understand that doing it will never make him "happy" in any conventional sense of the word: He must do the right thing for its own sake, not in the hope of any immediate reward. Significantly, he sees the potential for redemption in the men he kills, slaying them reluctantly and only after giving them a fair chance to change their ways. Sometimes the woman's weak husband dies in the crossfire, thus freeing her to fall in love with Scott, but in *Ride Lonesome* and *Comanche Station*, the best and most characteristic films of the series, he discharges his stern duty and rides off into the sunset without looking back, alone again and likely to remain so.

Redemption, on the other hand, is the whole point of the Boetticher-Scott films. It is what Scott is seeking, and what he hopes to offer to the warped half-heroes whom he meets on his endless pilgrimage. And though Boetticher shies away from overt religious symbolism—the cross-like hanging tree in *Ride Lonesome* is a rare exception—it is hard to fathom Scott's old-fashioned integrity without supposing that he believes in something beyond his own iron will. Why else would he insist on preserving his honor at the cost of his happiness?

Teachout's analysis is right on. The Scott-Boetticher-Kennedy protagonist is not a "white-hat" hero in the traditional Western-movie sense. He possesses a clearly defined—some might say rigid—code of honor but is not bound by the letter of the law. His code is simple and direct and makes no allowance for nuance; this is not a man who would spend time searching for the "root causes" behind an outlaw's depredations. He makes judgments about those with whom he comes into contact, but only insofar as their behavior affects his personal quest, or the people he has chosen to protect. And he allows the exigencies of a crisis to determine the extent to which he's willing to cooperate, and even assist, traveling companions who in other circumstances would be obvious enemies. He's hard, and sometimes cynical, but only because frontier life demands that of him. This protagonist respects women and quietly pines for the one he's lost, but he has little patience for female displays of overwrought emotionalism, and doesn't mind saying so.

The heavies are out-and-out rotters or once-decent people who have compromised their futures by allowing early mistakes to force them into lives of crime and venality. But even these antagonists aren't entirely devoid of traits that promote empathy. *The Tall T*'s Frank Usher expresses a liking of and admiration for Pat Brennan, and admits he has little in common with the cold-blooded Chink. *Ride Lonesome*'s Sam Boone and his partner Whit have criminal pasts but believe themselves redeemable, and although they anticipate clashing with Ben

Cody delivers Nancy Lane to her young son and blind husband at the end of *Comanche Station*.

Brigade over the killer Billy John, they agree to assist the bounty hunter when the boy's outlaw brother catches up with them at the clearing with the hanging tree. Even *Comanche Station*'s Ben Lane, destined for a showdown with Cody, can't bear to see his adversary ambushed by Indians and rides to the man's rescue.

While at odds with the elementary morality plays embodied in the Saturday-matinee "B" Westerns, these ambiguities of character more closely reflect real life and therefore constitute a large part of the appeal of the Ranown pictures written by Kennedy and directed by Boetticher.

The Alabama Hills and other settings in and around Lone Pine—including the sand dunes at Olancha and the meadows on the Spainhower ranch (fronting what is now Highway 395)—gave Boetticher and his cinematographers a starkly beautiful canvas on which to paint. Their framing of the rugged hills and majestic Sierra Nevada mountains suggest the relatively infinitesimal scale of the human drama— how tiny and insignificant the people seem!—while

at the same time imparting a mythic quality to the proceedings. Each long dusty trek captured in these movies is an Odyssey onto itself. The vastness of the setting treats the West as what one essayist called "a metaphoric space, an arena where competing value systems can be tested."

Lone Pine and the surrounding environs provided the scenic backdrop for hundreds of movies. Many were eminently forgettable, nothing more than formula quickies slated for Saturday-matinee screenings. Some, like *Gunga Din*, *High Sierra*, and *Bad Day at Black Rock*, had loftier ambitions and lived up to the expectations of discriminating moviegoers. But relatively few enjoy the sterling reputations of the Ranown Westerns of the late Fifties. And with good reason. Thankfully, these outstanding motion pictures can be seen easily: on Turner Classic Movies, on Encore's Westerns Channel, or on DVDs available from Sony Pictures Home Entertainment. They constitute important part of both the area's film history and the long-lived genre their excellence enhanced. ☐☐☐

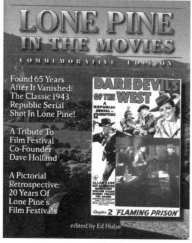
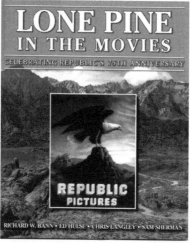
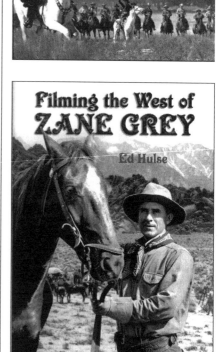
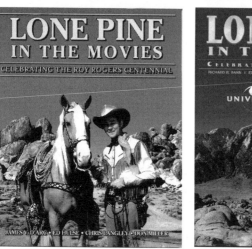
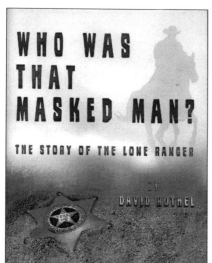

PHOTOGRAPHIC TREASURE HUNTING
IN THE ALABAMA HILLS

Many visitors and residents of Lone Pine, especially during festival weekend, have seen professional photographer Don Kelsen wandering in and around the rocks of the Alabama Hills. In pursuit of his passion to rediscover memorable movie locations with a group of friends, he painstakingly searches for and selects a vantage point using production stills and screen captures to duplicate with his camera some of the most spectacular visuals from our favorite Lone Pine films. His work continues on the following pages…

Above: Randolph Scott in scene from one of his Lone Pine films, photographed in pastoral setting on the Lubken Ranch, just south of Lone Pine. *Below:* John Wayne, in a scene from Republic's *Oregon Trail*, a "B"-Western title not seen since its original release in 1936. Wayne's character is John Delmont, a U.S. Army Captain who takes a leave of absence to find his missing father In the Alabama Hills.

Don Murray, 2012 Lone Pine Film Festival guest, visits area of the Alabama Hills where he worked in 1958 in the filming of *From Hell To Texas*. Murray stands in the same spot where, 54 years ago, he engaged in a gun battle with actor John Larch.

Don Murray, 2012 Lone Pine Film Festival guest, starred in *From Hell To Texas* (20th Century Fox, 1958), filmed in the Alabama Hills. Murray reacquaints himself with the rugged location, whose look has not changed in 54 years.

Billy King, 2013 Lone Pine Film Festival guest, is pictured at the railroad crossing in the opening scene of Hopalong Cassidy's *Heart of Arizona* (1938). The narrow gage railroad is long gone, the beautiful hills and surroundings remain the same at the foot of the Inyo Mountains, east of Lone Pine.

In the Hopalong Cassidy film *Secrets of the Wasteland* (1941) a scene representing the exit of a secret Chinese settlement is guarded by a member of a gang led by actor Douglas Fowley, whose goal is to steal the land from the Chinese.

Richard Boone starred as Paladin on television's *Have Gun Will Travel*. Boone takes cover behind rock in the Alabama Hills in this second-season episode from 1958, "The Road To Wickenberg."

Robbers are pursued by a posse through the rugged Alabama Hills in *The Last Posse* (1953), starring Broderick Crawford and John Derek.

Hopalong Cassidy, Brad King, and Andy Clyde ride into the sunset at the conclusion of *Secrets of the Wasteland* (1941), shot in the Alabama Hills.

Hopalong Cassidy and Topper in the Alabama Hills during production of *In Old Colorado* (1941).

Made in the USA
San Bernardino, CA
19 September 2013